S0-BEV-652

Senufo Sculpture from West Africa

1 Animal mask preceded by men carrying bows and arrows. Central region, Korhogo district, Kiembara fraction. Photo: P. Knops, s.m.a., 193

Senufo Sculpture from West Africa

by Robert Goldwater

The Museum of Primitive Art, New York

Distributed by New York Graphic Society

Greenwich, Connecticut 1964

15 West 54th Street
New York 19, New York

Printed in the United States of America
by Manhattan Art Press, Inc.

Library of Congress Card Number: 63-22414

For Jean-Louis

Foreword

The initial impulse for this monograph came from the task of gathering an exhibition of Senufo sculpture, shown first at The Museum of Primitive Art, and later at The Art Institute of Chicago and The Baltimore Museum. That exhibition was an opportunity to study and compare a large number of Senufo sculptures, and I am grateful to all the lenders, and to other museums and collectors who have also been most generous in furnishing information and photographs of their objects.

My indebtedness to the publications of those scholars who have worked among the Senufo is evident. But I wish especially to acknowledge the very friendly cooperation of several specialists: Dr. B. Holas of the Centre des Sciences Humaines, Abidjan, who responded to my questions and provided a useful annotated glossary of Senufo sculptured objects; Dr. Albert Maesen of the Musée Royal de l'Afrique Centrale, Tervuren, who permitted me to examine his unpublished dissertation and willingly answered further questions; Father P. Knops, s.m.a., who lived among the Senufo and generously sent the field photographs reproduced in the text; Mr. Gilbert Bochet, former administrator in the Ivory Coast, who contributed the drawings of masked dancers which are also illustrated. Mr. Emil Storrer kindly provided information on the rings of silence.

Mr. Adr. G. Claerhout of the Etnografisch Museum, Antwerp, Madame Jacqueline Delange of the Musée de l'Homme, Dr. A. A. Gerbrands of the Rijksmuseum voor Volkenkunde, Dr. Elsy Leuzinger of the Rietberg Museum, Dr. Roy Sieber of Indiana University, and Professor Dr. P. J. Vandenhoute of the Rijksuniversiteit, Gent were also most helpful in sending information on works in their respective museums. Mr. Eliot Elisofon and Mr. Walker Evans have kindly allowed the use of their photographs.

The realization of this volume was made possible by the whole staff of The Museum of Primitive Art. I wish to thank Miss Elisabeth Little for her checking of the manuscript, and Mr. Douglas Newton for his care with the book's layout and design. Mrs. Tamara Northern has helped throughout—with research and discussion; I am pleased to record her considerable contribution.

RG

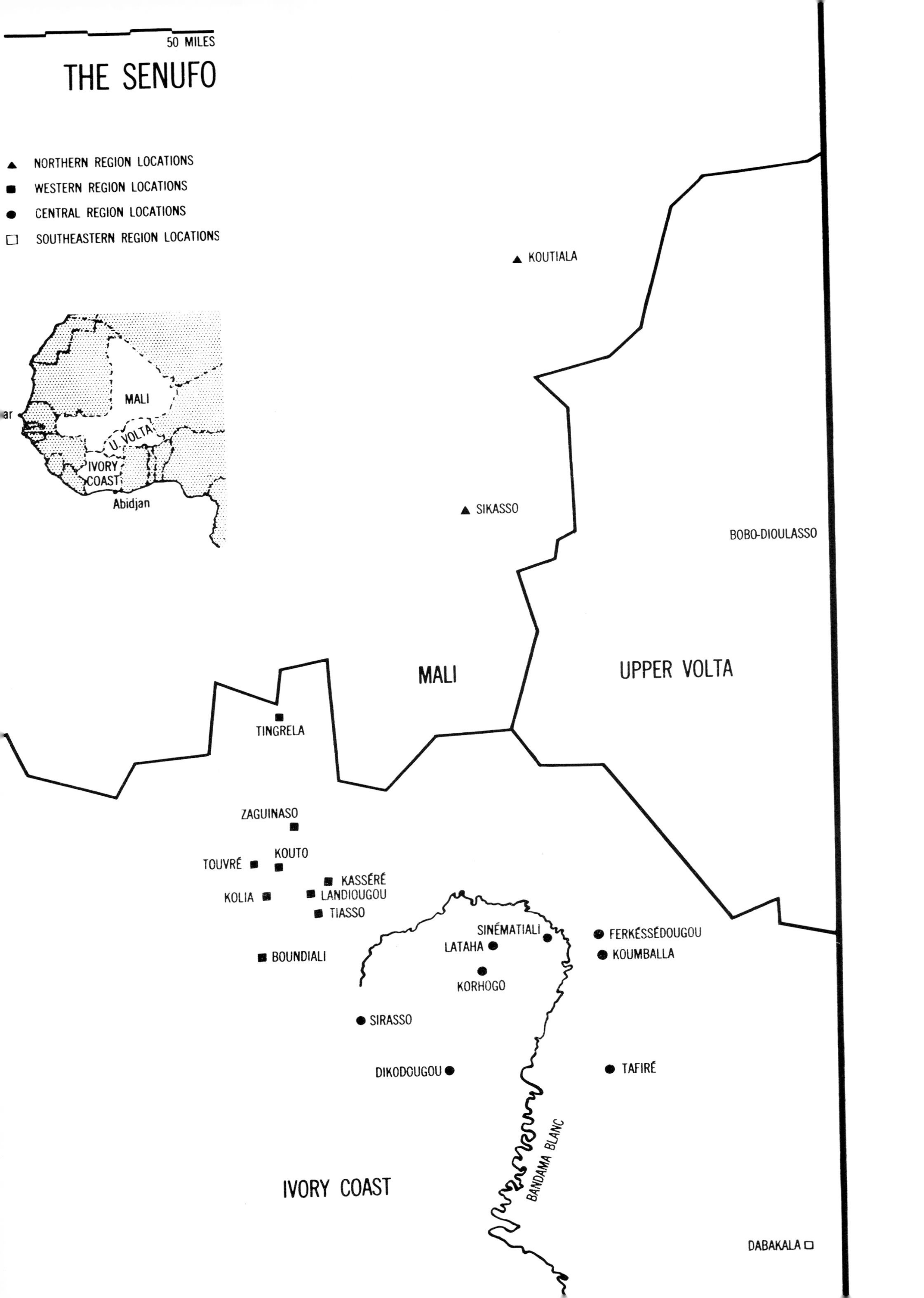
50 MILES
THE SENUFO
NORTHERN REGION LOCATIONS
WESTERN REGION LOCATIONS
CENTRAL REGION LOCATIONS
SOUTHEASTERN REGION LOCATIONS
MALI
U. VOLTA
IVORY COAST
Abidjan
KOUTIALA
SIKASSO
BOBO-DIOULASSO
MALI
UPPER VOLTA
TINGRELA
ZAGUINASO
TOUVRÉ
KOUTO
KASSÉRÉ
KOLIA
LANDIOUGOU
TIASSO
SINÉMATIALI
FERKÉSSÉDOUGOU
LATAHA
KOUMBALLA
BOUNDIALI
KORHOGO
SIRASSO
DIKODOUGOU
TAFIRÉ
BANDAMA BLANC
IVORY COAST
DABAKALA

2, 3 Villages in the northern Ivory Coast. Photos: Marc and Evelyne Bernheim, 1962

Illustrations

The numbers in the margins of the text refer to illustrations.

In the captions of the illustrations the following forms have been used to indicate grounds for assignment to style and provenance:

Direct information from field collectors	[F]
Indirect information and attributions by other collectors	[A]
Attributions on stylistic grounds by The Museum of Primitive Art	[S]

Senufo Sculpture from West Africa

The Senufo people, who together number nearly one million, live in an area that is today divided among the republics of the Ivory Coast, Mali and Upper Volta. Their neighbors to the south are the Baule and the Guro, to the southwest the Dan and the N'gere, to the northeast the Bobo, and along an extensive border to the north the Bambara, whose villages in the Sikasso area are interspersed with theirs. The arts of these peoples surrounding the Senufo (and of the more northerly Dogon) were already well known to the outside world at a time when little sculpture had come out of Senufo country. Partly for this reason, partly because their land (except for the Sudanese aspect of the region north of Sikasso), was neither clearly "coastal" nor clearly "steppe," Senufo art has often been described as "transitional," and placed somewhere between "round" and "pole" styles, or between naturalism and abstraction. But however helpful these broad categories may be for African art as a whole, such an easy summary of Senufo sculpture, emphasizing surrounding influences at the expense of inherent character, hardly does justice to the particular indigenous qualities of its style.

The Senufo did not always occupy their present territory. Following an earlier migration (still represented by the scattered residual groups of the Fodombélé), the main body of the population appears to have come from the north two or three hundred years ago. It is today divided into some twenty-five separate groups or "fractions," most densely gathered in the southern part of the area, in the general region of the large centers of Boundiali, Korhogo and Ferkessédougou.[1] The existence of these ethnic units is at least a partial explanation of the stylistic variations present within the clearly recognizable over-all character of Senufo art.

Primarily an agricultural people, the Senufo have had to get their subsistence from a poor land with the simplest of tools, using methods unchanged for many centuries. This fact helped to keep the social structure simple as well, and it is the village, made up of several extended families, that is the essential economic and political unit, owing no special allegiance to any larger, more centralized religious or secular organization. Each family within the village is in the nature of a "clan," all of its members having the same name, which is the name of their common mythical (animal or human) ancestor.

The importance of the soil may be indicated by the existence, alongside the village chief (who is himself considered a living ancestor, this being the source of his authority), of a "chief of the earth," who is the representative of the ancient founders of the village. "The earth, as traditionally conceived, is a collective and continuing good: it cannot belong [to anyone], because of its sacred character, which places it above the human level. The 'chief of the earth' . . . as manager of this inalienable heritage, is therefore primarily a *priest,* a person called to serve as intermediary between the two worlds, by means of the appropriate sacrificial acts. By virtue of this principle, the soil can only be the object of a *right of extended use* given to him who cultivates it;" it remains the property of the first ancestors.[2] It is thus natural that agricultural ceremonies, and the ritual carvings needed for them, should have a religious character.

The gods of the Senufo pantheon, as opposed to the ancestral spirits, play but a small part in their sculpture. The most important figures are "a creator god, a vague demiurge, once all-powerful, called Koulo Tyolo," and his feminine counterpart, Kâ Tyéléo, "literally mother-of-the-village, who is the great goddess of the group." Whereas Koulo Tyolo has no direct cult devoted to him, Kâ Tyéléo occupies an important liturgical role. "She is a great goddess of an essentially tellurian aspect, who also functions as a sublimation of the group in which she is incarnated;" and she acts as a mediator in the ritual of agrarian cults.[3] Although Kâ Tyéléo is basic to the rites of the lô society, neither she nor Koulo Tyolo are ever represented in art. It is the lesser spirits, as well as the ancestors, that are shown as figural sculpture.

The most important socio-religious institution of the Senufo is the lô society.[4] It exists in every village and gives a structure and unity beyond the closer ties of the family unit and the extended family. The lô is the kind of men's organization—similar to those existing in many primitive agricultural societies—that is generally called "secret" even though every adult male in the community eventually becomes a member. But the knowledge it holds and hands on from generation to generation is esoteric in that the young men must pass certain trials and initiations before it is imparted to them, and because it is (in principle) kept from all the women. The traditional secrets it possesses are in essence religious, related to the cosmology, the mythology, the ancestors and ancestral history of the Senufo. Because these traditions govern conduct, and because the lô functions as an age-grade society, in which all young men of the same group rise together through the various ranks, regardless of their family ties, the society plays an essential role in giving a cohesive framework to the social and political life of the village.

Although the organization of the lô varies in its details, such as the number of phases and their exact time-spans, its broad outlines seem to be the same everywhere. It is divided into three stages, or phases, each lasting seven years, and although sometimes subdivided, these are recognized as major divisions whose passage is marked by

4 Mask made of cowries, worn by the initiating elder of the lô society. Central region, Naffara fraction. Photo: P. Knops, s.m.a., 1935

initiations and ceremonies: The first group is that of the young boys; the second marks the stage of social adolescence; and the third belongs to manhood. Final graduation from this twenty-one year cycle takes place some time after the age of thirty, and in certain areas perhaps as late as between thirty-five and forty-five. This initiation at length accomplished, the Senufo man becomes part of the ruling "gerontocracy." "He belongs to 'the old men,' 'the wise men,' 'those who know,' to those whom the leaders consult on important religious, social and political decisions. From then on he is freed from communal agricultural labor, with the exception of certain tasks such as the nocturnal harvesting of millet, which are, rather, their privileges."[5]

The instruction given to the lô initiants has a double aspect, since it embraces both social and religious disciplines. But these are not really to be separated, as Holas emphasizes, since "among the Senufo perhaps even more than elsewhere, one can talk of the social function of religion," and "all social life is governed by precepts that are eminently religious."[6] Clearly, only a small portion of this long and gradual education is taken up with prescribed rites, which may last from a day to a month, and are separated by long working periods throughout each of the three seven-year phases. In the first, or prenubile stage, the disciplines are begun; obedience and tradition are taught through songs and dances. During the intermediate stage the

5 Headdresses worn by men preparing their initiation into the lô society. Central region, Korhogo district, Sinématiali village, Naffara fraction. Photo: P. Knops, s.m.a., 1935

enculturation process continues, and the adolescent (now given a temporary ritual name) is taught the "moral integration of the individual into the community," for whose sake he must henceforth be willing to sacrifice himself. He joins in communal work, learns ritual dances and songs, is introduced into army service, and after a terminal period of solitude and trial, lasting several weeks, graduates with the other members of his age-group into the adult stage.[7] He now participates in major ceremonies that teach a deeper understanding of the mythical and religious tradition, learns the special language of the lô, incomprehensible to outsiders, and is given his definitive secret name. The ceremonies of this last phase (called tyologo among both the Naffara and Kiembara fractions), are carried out in the sinzanga, the sacred wood or grove.

Each Senufo village has its sinzanga, situated on its outskirts, and perhaps marking the location of the original settlement.[8] It is a spot forbidden to all but the properly qualified lô initiates, concealed from the profane so that they may not penetrate the secrets of the society. Father Knops has published a view of the grove of the village of Sinématiali showing, behind a circle of logs used as seats by the initiants, several huts for the safekeeping of ritual objects.[9] Father Clamens, who was able to visit some twenty different groves, also mentions these huts, from which, on one occasion, a group of masks and figures were brought out for him to photograph.[10] While these works, and others that he enumerates, are wooden sculptures of the types found in museum collections, older descriptions also emphasize pottery images that are rarely seen outside Senufo country. Thus 6 Delafosse, in 1908, mentions rough clay representations of human figures and crocodiles which "decorate several sacred groves," while Vendeix, describing the groves as they had been shortly after 1900 says, "They were furnished with statues or effigies in red clay representing all the 'totems' of the family: buffalo, panthers, crocodiles, snakes, antelopes, form a fantastic population designed to strike the imagination. . . . Today [1934] the sacred groves are less mysterious . . . the initiating ceremonies comprise rather complicated ritual dances. The dancers are dressed according to the inclination of the village. While some have helmets made of cowries, topped by boards like 'sandwich' men, others have big cotton hoods ornamented with cowry designs that seem to imitate certain birds. Several have enormous masks of bombax wood representing all sorts of animals, and certain virile attributes, all old, dirty, and sometimes repelling. . . . In a language unknown to the non-initiate the members of the lô society, in the depths of the sacred grove, celebrate their ancestral cult, praise the souls of their forefathers, and ask them to watch over and protect the poor creatures now alive."[11]

The observations of Holas, made many years later, bear out the importance the Senufo give to the souls of their ancestors. "All the acts of the [lô]," he says, in reality only carry out the wishes of the ancestors: they preside, in some way, at all agrarian rites . . . the basic ceremony of the social year is the burial rites organized in honor of the dead." Nevertheless, this cult is not the foundation of Senufo religion, "since the souls of the dead . . . are never confused with the divine essences, nor with the other 'occult' entities and consequently cannot be included in the Senufo pantheon."[12]

On the other hand, the social importance of the lô is indicated by the fact that marriages are legal only when the husband has been inducted into its second seven-year phase (known as kwonro), and that its presence is necessary for the funerary ceremonies validly separating the dead from the living so that they truly become useful ancestors rather than harmful ghosts. In summing up the lô, Holas describes it as "a microcosm, a reduced and sublimated version of the group, and at the same time a condenser of social energy providing all the values indispensable to the perpetuation of life and the maintenance of order."[13] It is only natural that this importance should be reflected in Senufo art: we will see that the most impressive of the sculptures are connected with the rites of the lô society.

Among the Senufo, as generally among the peoples of West Africa, the artisan occupies a special place. He is usually referred to in the literature as a blacksmith—but this term must be understood in its oldest and widest sense—and he belongs to a special group, or caste, largely endogamic, which is separate from the main body of Senufo farmers. Nevertheless he must cultivate his own fields, deriving his living only partly from his technical specialty, as is the case also among the neighbors of the Senufo. That specialty includes the fashioning of all objects made from metal: agricultural tools, weapons, knives used in the sacrificial killing of animals, amulets, divination figures, and masks. But it is not merely a craft knowledge of metal-working skills that gives the artisan his place apart; this is established rather by his inseparable and magic connection with fire and the forces of earth inherent in the extracted metal. Thus, as Father Knops points out, to be a blacksmith is not simply to have learned a métier; rather, one is a blacksmith "in essence," born as such, and remaining so whether or not he practices the profession.[14] "The forge is a sacred place," says Holas, "the sanctuary of tellurian forces at once feared and indispensable to the harmonious functioning of human society. . . . Thus everything that comes from the hand of the blacksmith carries the 'fluid' of a consecrated object."[15] The supernatural powers which are his by birth, explains Father Knops, he transmits to the things he makes "communicating the forces which belong to other powers that he tries to influence so that they will make the family or the tribe to which the blacksmith belongs participate in their beneficial virtues, or drive away malignant influence."[16]

Being by nature different from the other Senufo, although apparently part of the original population, it is understandable that the blacksmiths (fonombélé) should live apart.[17] They may inhabit their own villages, or be spread out as separate units attached to the various "quarters" of a larger town, each made up of an extended family.[18] The blacksmiths also have their own lô, whose rites are similar to the farmers' lô, and which may either make use of the same sacred grove, or have its own alongside. Perhaps because the knowledge and virtue it teaches are vital to their craft, the final initiation into the stage of maturity takes place—much earlier than with the farmers—some time before the age of twenty-five.[19]

There is some difference of opinion as to whether the wood carvers constitute a caste separate from the metal workers. Father Knops, whose very detailed descriptions of the role and the techniques of the Senufo artisan are based on many years' observation, does not separate them: "The professional competence [of the blacksmiths] extends to the working of wood, ivory, clay, stone, gourds and coconut shell." "He extracts and prepares the minerals, forges or casts metal, shapes and carves wood, while the women of the caste mold pottery."[20] The woodworker does have a special name (navaga), and is more given to black magic, but he functions within the same caste as the metalworker. Similarly Lem, whose observations also go back to the 'thirties, in describing both the Senufo and their immediate neighbors, says, "These craftsmen, who have never ceased to be tillers of the soil . . . are at the same time smiths, woodcarvers and potters."[21]

More recent investigators, however, have divided metalworkers and woodcarvers into distinct castes, and restrict the term koulé, to woodcarvers alone. Thus Himmelheber, gathering his information in the Korhogo region "was explicitly told that the koulé was not merely a branch of the smiths, that had devoted itself entirely to carving. No, the koulé had never had anything to do with iron." Holas, who points out the excellence of the women potters, finds even more specialized groupings. He distinguishes the caster or jewelry-maker (lorho), who is a specialist in copper, from the blacksmiths (fonombélé) in general, and also differentiates between the koulé who are "a group of artisans who work with wood," and the "specialists grouped as a more or less endogamic 'caste'—the daleubélé or kpémbélé" who execute the Senufo statues.[22] Perhaps these more exclusive groupings are the result of a recent accelerated evolution.

The special position of the Senufo artisan results in a special attitude towards him. As with his neighbors the Bambara (but very differently from the Bakuba and the Yoruba, for example) he is at once "looked down upon and feared by the population," as Lem puts it; or in the words of Father Knops, "because of the magical practices to which they are given, as much as their skills which are indispensable to the life of the group . . . it is not surprising that the artisans are *feared*. In many instances this fear degenerates into disdain. . . ." Holas considers "disdain" (also found by Himmelheber, who could discover no reason for it) an inaccurate description of the "bipolar

6 Pottery vessel. Clay with grass binder, cowry eyes, 20½" high. Ex collection Robert Stolper, New York

7 Pottery making. Southern region, Katiola district, Tagwana fraction. Photo: P. Knops, s.m.a., 1934

feeling shown by profane opinion" toward the artisan, in which "many reservations of a social nature are always mixed with a more or less respectful apprehension."[23]

The artisan caste, perhaps the survivors of an older population, spared by comparatively recent invaders precisely because of their special knowledge, and still respected and feared because of it, nevertheless occupies a low position in the social scale well below that of the farmer, and in a certain way below that of the slave, who after all once had a higher status. At the same time, and partly because of the singular position he occupies, the artisan indulges in questionable magic, thus reinforcing the ambiguous sentiments that are the natural result of his special relation to the forces he channels.

This then is the social context in which the Senufo sculptor carries on his work, making the face and helmet masks, the large and small figures needed for the initiation rites of the lô society, for funerals and commemorative ceremonies, for the dances banishing soul-eaters and for divination procedures. His techniques are those of the West African sculptor generally.[24] He uses an adze and a knife to carve the freshly cut wood, which while still green is easier to work. He employs a variety of species, usually softer woods for the large animal helmet masks (for which the bombax tree is most commonly employed), harder woods for the smaller face masks and for figures. Surfaces are smoothed by rubbing with rough leaves, and patination given by the successive application of karite butter and smoking, which darkens and preserves the wood (castor oil is also used), or by adding a coat of kaolin, either partially or over all, which whitens it. Of the other colors red is the most usual, contrasting with the white to create spotted patterns on animals masks, or lozenge designs on the large bird carvings. The addition of red kisi seeds or white cowry shells fixed by natural gums (frequent among the neighboring Bambara) seldom occurs, but the cloth and raffia costumes worn with the masks are often many-hued. The Senufo metal techniques are also those common to West Africa as a whole: brass or bronze of varying composition is cast by the lost wax method to produce a solid metal form. The relative roles played by tradition and individual innovation are here, as elsewhere, difficult if not impossible to determine, although the "fractioning" of the Senufo people has an undoubted bearing on variations of style. But it is clear that the distinctive character of

8 Kpélié. Drawing by Gilbert Bochet

9 Koutopitya (an avatar of the kpélié). Drawing by Gilbert Bochet

their art is not dependent upon any materials or methods particular to them or different from those of their neighbors. The sources of Senufo style—and its historical changes, could we but trace them—must be found in the fusion, or the interaction, of iconographic purpose and esthetic sense.

Face Masks

The Senufo face mask is in many ways a kind of paradigm of African sculptural style. Though it is small (being just barely large enough to cover the face), finely cut, and intricate in design, it possesses a 21 total strength well beyond the delicacy of each detail. Its features are of obvious naturalistic derivation, yet it is clearly not even a generalized rendering of the observed human face, much less ever an individual portrait. It combines an effect of energy that suggests the movement and activity of ritual context with a trance-like rigidity of expression. And its various examples, within the strict limits of a traditional style and iconography, achieve a wide range of effective design.

Nevertheless, the face mask, though it is almost always recognizably Senufo, cannot simply be said to be typical of Senufo style. Its small size and fine execution are unlike the large and boldly-featured animal 22 helmet masks. Its ornamental complication is very different from the undecorated simplicity of both the large and small figure sculptures. Its clean edge carving of the narrow, sharply-cut nose and projecting mouth bears a relation to the mask style of the neighboring Guro, and although the Senufo handling usually exposes the teeth in an oval, open mouth that thrusts straight forward (which the Guro never does) there is perhaps a stylistic affinity.

What is exceptional here, however, is an agglomeration of elements. The face itself, relatively pure in its stylized naturalism, has a smooth surface set off by the raised welt patterns of tribal, or "caste," markings, a surface which the wearer rubs with chewed kola nuts before and after the dance.[25] But its features are set in the midst of a collection of disparate iconographic elements only some of which can be accounted for. Some of the ornamentation can perhaps be explained as an elaboration of coiffure, though it has come a long way from its source.[26] This would seem to be the origin of the curved striations over and to each side of the forehead, and, less surely, of the oval or rectangular shapes, usually marked with repeated ridges, that jut out on either side. Those examples in which these patterns are carried 23 around the top of the forehead would seem to bear this out, but when these projecting forms are dropped lower, as they often are, they lose even this suggestion of meaning. At the top is an heraldic repre- 24 sentation—a row of palm nuts, a bird, a chameleon, or a human figure —that indicates the mask belongs to a certain group or caste. But the most common features are the rams horns, which appear alone 25 or accompanied by the central element, and they remain unexplained.

The lower portions of the design that frames the face are less obvious. At the height of the cheeks or slightly lower there is usually, but not always, a triangle or a semi-ellipse, which is either a solid plane or worked into an open design. Here reasons of decorative symmetry, balancing the upper portions, would seem to be at work. Beneath this, and extending below the narrow chin, is a pair of what appear to be legs, and which are so referred to by the Senufo themselves, although no reason has been given for their appearance in this context (the mask, attached to its costume, is not held by them as has been sometimes suggested.)[27] On the analogy of the Bakota guardian figures one might suggest that they symbolize the body, which disappears after death, although the parallel is not exact. It is also possible that they represent birds' legs, and some, in fact, are rather accurate, naturalistic renderings. In this case they would refer to the recurrent symbol of fertility, the hornbill, either being all that remains of a once complete representation, or on a *pars pro toto* principle found elsewhere in Senufo iconography.[28]

The face mask is an ancestor mask. Although some examples show the lip-plug, which is a feminine adornment, it is not this detail (or 23 its absence) which determines the sex of the mask, but its ritual context and the appropriate decorations added to the costume at the moment of its use.[29] The mask has various names (kpélié, kodélié, kpéligué) said to be synonymous, but Maesen reports that near Korhogo it was known as kulíe.[30] He derives this name from ku = the dead, and íe = the face, and suggests this indicates that originally the mask was always an ancestor mask used religiously, and that the purely recreative function it occasionally had was the result of a later evolution toward the secular, of a not uncommon type.

The mask has a variety of functions. It takes part in the rites of the lô society on different occasions: at initiation ceremonies, at funerary and second burial rites for lô members, and it also is employed at harvest festivals when thanks are given to ancestors who have helped to ensure good crops. But the mask also appears outside the confines of the lô when it functions as the common property of a female community; in this slightly different context (it still refers to ancestors), its form remains the same.

Such interchangeability does not apply to the heraldic emblems that top many of the masks. These elements mark the mask as belonging to a particular group of a given area—a crest for the farmers, palm nuts for the sculptors, a bird-figure for the blacksmiths, a human figure for the Dioula (a Mandé people) who are generally traders—and limit the use of the mask to that one group.[31] As has been noted, however, the most general feature is the pair of horns, which may appear alone, or coupled with one of the group emblems, or in some examples placed and shaped to represent both horns and outstretched wings of the bird emblem. The horns are generally rams horns, turned down and coming forward over the plane of the mask, but strongly vertical, upward-pointing horns (probably of antelope origin) also occur and the difference is not, it would appear, a matter of geographical distribution, since both types are found in the same region.

Interpretations of the exact meaning of these ancestor masks differ. Maesen tells us that it is the first two age-grades of the lô which wear them and that they are very much feared when worn at the funerary rites of lô society members.[32] Holas, who remarks on the aspect of spirituality and meditation says that the kpélié evokes a metaphysical concept which is progressively revealed to those who enter into the higher levels (tiologo and kafo) after painful initiations "the particular purpose of the kpélié is to recall to the neophyte the imperfection and precariousness of the human condition."[33]

Double masks also appear, whose joined faces are necessarily longer and narrower than the single-visage form. They may have a single or 26 a double crest above, and two or four legs below. These masks are said to represent the male and female principles of the universe, joined in a reference to fertility and increase; yet even here the feminine lip-plug, which might be thought a necessary feature of one of 27 the joined countenances, is not necessarily present, since its known meaning does not depend upon this kind of representational determinant.[34]

If one is to judge on the basis of the precisely documented examples (and there would seem to be no other way to proceed) the central region produced the most numerous and, in a sense, the most typical face masks. The characteristic style of this area is given by a mask 29 collected by Maesen (1938) in the Korhogo district, whose details of style are almost exactly repeated in a similar mask collected by Storrer in 1949. With only slight variations many others resemble these in 30 proportion, finish, and the rather sturdy, large-scale handling of the ornament surrounding the face. From the village of Kokwo in this same region comes another example collected by Maesen with a more elongated face, a greater separation of the flanking decoration, and the especially striking open loop work. With its smooth surface (whose absence elsewhere may be partly due to the accidents of preservation) it has an uncommon lightness and grace.[35] These same loops and narrow proportions are found in another more elaborate mask with a large superstructure of patterned horns and a crest, that fortunately still preserves the attached antelope horns and feathers and a portion of the hemp costume that covered its wearer; in this setting the face seems even more removed from an everyday reality. Thus the style of the central region contains a variety of emphases.

An entirely different style of face mask was collected by Lem in the Bobo-Dioulasso district in the northern region of the Senufo area.[36] The crest above the forehead, the head decoration itself, the flanking projections, rectangular, rounded or triangular, and the projecting legs, all these are characteristically Senufo. But here the human brows and eyes, and what seems the beginning of a human nose and cheeks run smoothly into a long and graceful bird's beak. The result is unexpected but sculpturally convincing. Unlike other Senufo sculpture (except perhaps in its stress on the recurrent bird motif), it cannot be explained by the influence of any neighboring styles, which contain no similar forms of stylization. Nor can we be sure to what extent its comparative rarity is due merely to the accidents of collecting.

The southeastern region, the area around Katiola and Dabakala, is the source of still another stylistic variation of the face mask. As one would expect in this region where Senufo and Baule peoples intermingle, it is of a more naturalistic aspect, with rounder proportions, a broader nose, and a mouth which though still small and projecting, does not show the teeth in the manner of the central region convention. The surrounding ornament (or iconography) has been greatly reduced and is now confined to the upper part of the face and forehead, so that it seems a simple extension of the hair arrangement that has been built up over the face, sometimes in two-, sometimes in three-dimensional fashion. Especially, the "legs" have disappeared, or have perhaps been raised, reduced and joined to the decorative patterns at the sides of the face. As long ago as 1898 Richard Austin Freeman illustrated a mask very like Fig. 34 which he described as a "sacrobundi mask of polished black wood from Jimini" [i.e., Djimini fraction], and we thus have evidence that this style has some antiquity.[37] Some masks of this type, which are reliably said to be old specimens, have applied metal ornament, in the form of bands, disks, lozenges, and round-headed tacks distributed at intervals over the wood surface. This kind of metal appliqué resembles certain Bambara or Marka masks, and is probably due to the influence of the Dioula who live scattered throughout this area and up into the Korhogo region.[38] Despite differences of detail and treatment of the hair these masks clearly belong to a stylistically related group.

In the matter of both style and usage, the metal face masks present a more difficult problem. There are some, undoubtedly fairly old, which closely resemble the wooden masks. The metal mask given to Father Knops from the Treasure of King Fandio at Sinématiali has the characteristics of the wooden masks of that region, and the mask in the Leiden museum is even more typical, its mouth (filled with teeth), horns and legs closely resembling, for instance, a wooden mask in the Musée de l'Homme known to come from the Korhogo area. And there are others which imitate the applied ornaments scattered on the surface of some of the southeastern region masks that have been discussed above. This is clearly the case for one of the two metal masks in The Museum of Primitive Art, where casting and finish are both rough, even though the star and crescent motif derives from Islam; and it may be true as well of the other more regular more nearly-designed example. There are also, however, instances of metal masks in a much less traditional style, with certain elements of uncharacteristic fantasy, notably in the shape of the legs and the application of decoration to them, the generous distribution of imaginative scarification, and untraditional mouths and eyes. One can only conclude that these are "strongly acculturated" and of recent date.

There remains the question of whether the metal masks were ever used ceremonially. Holas thinks it doubtful, and there are many reasons for agreeing with him.[39] The fact that most of them came from the central region, yet exhibit a variety of style and iconography well beyond that of the wooden masks, suggests particularly that they are one remove away from any immediate socio-religious function.

Helmet Masks

While the best of the Senufo face masks are distinguished by an almost miniature-like conception, quite the opposite is true of their helmet masks. Almost all of the several kinds are characterized by a broken, bristling silhouette made up of an assortment of jaws, teeth, ears and horns put together on a large scale and executed with vigor. This is not to say, in the language of older commentators, that they are "crude," meaning that they do not reach an acceptable level of craftsmanship (and naturalism).[40] Quite the opposite is the case. Composing so iconographically complicated and visually intricate a program from a single block of wood requires sculptural imagination and

10 Kponiougo. Drawing by Gilbert Bochet

11 Waniougo. Drawing by Gilbert Bochet

12 Korubla. Drawing by Gilbert Bochet

technical planning, all carried out with attention to detail and surface. But it is immediately evident that whatever ideas their parts may embody, these masks are intended to be taken in at a single glance, that they are meant to impress, and to terrify. And this is, in fact, their functional role.

The ceremonial purpose and the visual effect are therefore very different from those of the delicate face mask, and this range and variety is one of the characteristics of Senufo sculpture. Yet in the manner of their conception there is a certain similarity, for both face and helmet masks consist of a gathering together of separate, and naturalistically incongruous elements. In the face mask there is a juxtaposition of human and "abstract" components; while here, although each of the parts is drawn directly from nature, they are not to be found together in the natural world. The most common of the animal masks, whose prominent features are its single muzzle and long horns (the type that has come to be known as "firespitter"), can include iconographic details taken from the buffalo, the wart hog, the crocodile and the antelope, in its larger parts, plus small representations of a chameleon and a bird, even sometimes a snake. It would seem correct to say that this sort of additive compositional imagination is more characteristic of Senufo art than of other African styles.

It serves, at any rate, to emphasize an important fact about these masks: what they depict (i.e., the sources they stem from in nature), is very different from what they finally represent (i.e., the ideas they embody in ceremonial use).[41] It is perhaps quite clear that this must be true of the imaginatively constructed creature of the usual firespitter, but one must remember that it applies as well to the simpler forms without horns that are derived from the baboon or from the hyena. The intention of all of them is the same: ceremonially, these are demons rather than animals; and, while they are in use at least, they fuse with the demon, or his spirit with them, and temporarily become his embodiment.

In their added details the iconographic allusion of these masks carries further, so as to connect them with the recurrent body of Senufo mythology. Crowning the helmet portion of most of the horned masks, whether of the single or double-muzzled variety, and of many of the hornless ones as well, are one or more small representations, whose size is no measure of their importance: there is the familiar hornbill, symbol of fertility, and the associated masculine symbol of the python, whose form may be abstracted into a sinuous line; there is the chameleon, which by its "hesitant and cautionary walk recalls the undifferentiated mud of the primordial universe"; and finally there is 52 the little cup (often supported by hornbill and chameleon), which "is filled with a special substance supposed to guarantee the efficacy of the ritual."[42] It is this cup, or perhaps the material that fills it, which 57 is called wa, that gives the masks that carry it their name of waniougo. 11 The waniougo, Holas informs us, is a special form of this type of mask whose more general name, applied as well to versions without the cup, 10 is kponiougo, meaning "head" or "countenance" of the lô. He assigns to the mask a mythological and practical role similar to that of the sacred statues; "[it serves as] a connecting link between humanity and the amorphous universe of the ancestors on the one hand, and between humanity and its protecting gods on the other."[43] It plays an essential role in agricultural, initiatory and funeral ceremonies.

Two older descriptions of these animal masks assign them a somewhat different role. Prouteaux in 1914, and Maesen in 1938, concluded that the chief function of the masks is the driving away of soul eaters.[44] They connect them primarily with secret societies (which vary from place to place) other than the lô, and agree that though these or very similar masks also appear at funeral ceremonies of members of the society they are not in the first instance funerary masks. The purpose of the mask is always to inspire fear; it has such great power that even the initiates must observe certain taboos in handling it; touching its costume during its appearance may be dangerous even for the initiated, while its sight for a non-initiate, and particularly for any woman, will cause sickness and possibly death.[45]

Prouteaux was present at the dance of one of these horned masks, which he calls gbon, and describes it in some detail. The dancer, who was required to be nude under his ritual costume was hidden by a large mantle of raffia braids which came down to his knees, and his legs were covered by trousers of a rough material. The gbon appeared at night after the population had been gathered by the drumming of young boys, who also sang gaily as they waited for his entrance. The mask, accompanied by drums, trumpets and chanting, and the more piercing sound of a sort of flail, held a leather whip as he walked and turned, sometimes on tiptoe, and sometimes on his knees. "At his approach everyone kneeled and bent down, their eyes fixed on the fringes of his costume spread out by his pirouettes, and whose touch they had to avoid . . . ; [but the sorcerers] hypnotized by the devilish music of the adepts, and by the presence of the spirit in the village, cannot hold still, and are driven out."[46] The gbon is said to have superhuman powers: it can seat itself unharmed on a fire of glowing coal, which will then be put out; with a single bound it can climb into a tree or on top of a house; it can throw sparks through the straw roof of a sorcerer's hut without setting it on fire.

But the most curious practice of the gbon, says Prouteaux, is firespitting. From time to time, the gbon "lets fall down his costume two fist-fulls of sparks and tiny glowing coals which rapidly die out on touching the ground. These jets of flame are very skillfully executed, and make a great impression on the audience. Certainly it is paradoxical to have fire fall across a curtain of hemp without anything catching on fire, and the supply of embers is large enough so that half an hour after [the mask's] entrance it has not been used up."[47]

Maesen describes the mask's appearance in the evening, as prepared for by a ritual that includes its painting with red and white earth colors both spread and spotted, the attachment of small goat horns as magic containers, and the insertion of bird feathers.[48] Because the mask must be put in a good mood for the pursuit of the soul-eaters, it is offered sacrifices both before and after the chase. In his observation, the masks do not execute a dance but rather simply walk and run. At a certain point they disappear into the bush, and thence give forth roaring cries as a sign of victory at having surprised a soul-eater. He also witnessed the firespitting performance of the demon "who blows sparks through the muzzle of the mask and, on some occasions, ends his performance dancing barefooted upon a pile of burning logs until they are extinguished." "Before setting out in the open savannah, at night, the masks ran through the outskirts of the village. They were part of a small band of society members roaring incantations and drumming. From time to time the mask wearer shouted formulas in a high-pitched tone, and proceeded to blow out a small blast of glowing sparks and little flames. This was produced by means of grass properly cut in tiny pieces and smeared with a sort of resin also used in torches. The mixture was ignited from inside the jaws of the mask by the bearer blowing upon a small but heavily ash-coated piece of smouldering wood from the marrow core of a tree."[49]

Maesen notes that although the function of the helmet mask is invariable its name alters according to the local organization to which it belongs, and its representational features are also changeable. As Prouteaux uses gbon to refer to these masks generally, so Maesen (as well as Himmelheber) employs korubla as a generic appellation. Both 12 Holas and Bochet, however, indicate that korubla is a much more specific name designating a hornless mask without the cup, or wa, on its 60 forehead, and depicting a baboon.[50] This is a funerary mask, much more closely connected with the lô society and its initiation ceremonies. It is worn with a cynocephalic mane, and the dancer carries a double membrane drum on his chest; it is fitted out with feathers, and with bundles of porcupine quills and the dried bodies of hedgehogs. There are two types of korubla masks. In one, the animal alone is represented, so that despite the convention of the joined teeth, 61 the naturalistic source is quite evident (Leiden and Seattle). 62 In the other (British Museum), 55 by a different treatment of eyebrows and eyeball, and by the addition of a projection below the nose which is referred to as a mouth (as distinct from the jaws) a human face has, as it were, been laid over the animal muzzle. This fusion is found in other korubla examples which are all without horns although they may 56 carry the chameleon or the hornbill; it is also typical of the horned masks, whether or not they have the magic cup.

Given their primary demonological intention, and the mixture of sources that has already been noted, any inquiry into the specific animal from which each of these masks derives may not seem pertinent. On the one hand the artist has had his rendering severely limited by tradition; on the other a good deal of imagination has gone into the creation of that tradition: on both scores exact transcription suffers. But this morphological problem is linked with that of geographical distribution and provenance.

The characteristic "firespitter," documented by the Prouteaux photographs (1914), the Bochet drawings, and the "dated" examples in Paris, Antwerp and the collection of Mrs. Frans Olbrechts—the type 57 that occurs most frequently—comes from the central region. Apart from the features on the crown, which may include either or both antelope and rams horns, these masks have a double set of tusks, one out of the nose and one out of the jaws, which suggest a wart hog. This applies equally to single and double-faced examples, although where the nose is very narrow and the jaw very wide (Paris) there 52 may also be a suggestion of the waterbuck. Maesen, who worked in the central region, refers to a boar mask with horns, and Lem, near Korhogo, collected a hornless mask with one set of tusks in the jaws which he describes as the "boar-man."[51] Lem also found two "hyena" masks, one single, the other double, which have directly carved on 63 them the small goat horns that are usually attached, in the Folona district in the north.[52] The considerable stylization of this type is in line with the tendency toward abstraction generally held to be characteristic of the more northerly areas. Thus another, rarer type of bovine helmet mask (also first collected by Lem in the 'thirties) has on these 66 grounds been attributed to the northern Senufo area.[53] Where then is one to place the provenance of the double mask in the Deskey col- 68 lection, one of whose muzzles is of the typical central region type, while the other has the wide flap-jaw and withdrawn teeth found in the Folona examples? The association in one work of two apparently distinct tendencies once more suggests that mutual influences were more widespread than we have been wont to assume, and that one must not be overly rigid in associating a given style with a single region.

Kagba and Nassolo

There is still another, reduced version of the animal helmet mask. As it turns up in western collections divested of its attendant costume, with elegant proportions, carefully executed detail, and a headpiece 70 apparently too small to be worn, it looks as if it might be a "non-functional" work of art. It is slim and drawn out, with ringed antelope horns that sweep up and rams horns that bend down, a small chameleon on the forehead, and a long, thin snout that projects from a narrowed 71 section at the face. But it clearly cannot be worn in the usual manner of the helmet mask. Here is a striking instance in which knowledge of context is indispensable for any understanding not only of a work's intent and function, but also of its original visual effect.

What that was may best be grasped from the drawing by Bochet, 13 which we reproduce. This shows the wooden mask as the small head of a much larger body, the whole known as kagba (house of the village). The wearer, naked beneath his covering, carries a large tent-like structure made of a liana framework on which has been stretched a surface of palm leaves painted with symbolic geometric designs in white, black and ochre, or in blue and white. At one gable peak is the wooden, sculptured head, at the other a raffia tail. Only lô society initiates may view the kagba, which is its symbol; to others it brings death, so that when it is carried in funeral ceremonies people take refuge in their houses. Then, Father Knops tells us, "a sinister silence descends on the village, broken only by the regular, lugubrious droning of the rhomb . . . which produces a sound like the lowing of a bull . . . The kagba's cortege is impressive: two men, . . . masked by a cloth stretched in a triangle, and armed with a whip, precede it while they produce a shrill whistling sound."[54]

One of these masked attendants, dressed in a spotted costume that covers him completely, may be seen in a photograph taken at Sinémat- 69 iali which shows what Holas has described as an improved form of the kagba, known as nassolo, a word literally transcribed as "buffalo-elephant," i.e., a buffalo the size of an elephant. The nassolo is some ten feet long, to the six of the kagba; it is rounded rather than triangular in section; and its increased size requires it to be carried by

13 Kagba. Drawing by Gilbert Bochet

14 Kwonro. Drawing by Gilbert Bochet

two men. It, too, has a carved animal's head at one end, and a noise-making apparatus manipulated on the interior. Bochet describes the nassolo as "a remarkable attempt to group together the largest possible number of symbolic elements in order to suggest the totality of the initiation sequence and structure."[55] This applies to the kagba as well, and it is noteworthy that these masks are confined to the Naffara fraction of the Senufo, in the districts of Ferkessédougou and Sinématiali, and that the Naffara add to the three usual stages of lô society initiations, a fourth, higher level, which they call kagba.[56] Thus both mask and grade are a kind of summing up.

Kwonro

The initiation procedures of the lô society spanned long periods, with ceremonies held at intervals, and the final rites of acceptance into the senior grade being enacted only once every seven years. The induction of the postulants into the intermediate (or adolescent) phase, called Kwonro, that preceded full membership employed a mask consisting of a wooden or wicker cap supporting a flat stylized decoration. It was worn with a special costume, as shown in the drawing by Bochet, who remarks that it was "characterized by a great wealth of plastic invention and a great dogmatic void, a weakness which caused it to be among the first [ceremonial costumes] to disappear in the recent evolution of society."[57] Father Knops also has described "the dancing processions in which the postulants are dressed in wooden helmets topped by a small board carved in a black and white checkerboard pattern, or in more or less stylized birds or reptiles, and dressed with crossed cords and a belt, all in cotton sewn with cowries, and each one carrying a horsetail in his right hand. All of these accessories had a merely decorative purpose."[58] Although none of these descriptions mention figure decoration, there is one similarly shaped wooden cap mask surmounted by a horse and rider (carved in a style that suggests a northern provenance) that may also have been employed in the kwonro ceremony.

Two other larger masks may also be mentioned here, since their wooden caps indicate that they were worn in the same way. They have much more elaborate openwork patterns, with a symbolic repertory that includes the familiar animals of creation and increase (bird, tor-

15 Déguélé. Drawing by Gilbert Bochet

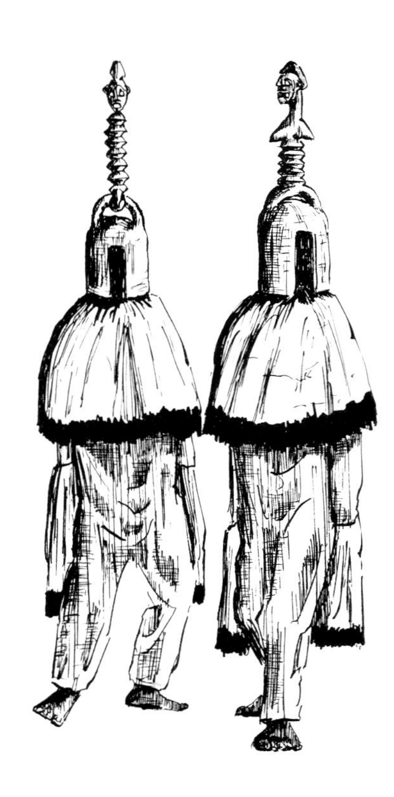

toise and snake) as well as figures and masks, which are also found in the relief carving on drums and doors.[59] This, as well as their size, suggests a more important ceremonial function than the kwonro, and they are perhaps rather to be compared to the large bird sculptures, the porpianong, which standing on similar hollowed-out caps, were 150 carried on heads of members during lô society rituals.

Déguélé

In 1939 Maesen, after his year of field work among the Senufo, brought back from the village of Kolewo, near Korhogo—a region inhabited by the Kiembara fraction—a pair of helmet masks topped by armless figures, one male, the other female, with strange abstract bodies. These masks, to which Maesen gave no name, are today in the Antwerp 82 museum and the Ethnographic Collections of The University of Ghent. In 1953 Father Clamens, as part of an article describing the sacred grove of the lô society, made the first published reference to this same kind of helmet mask.[60] He visited twenty such groves, and in one of them (which he prudently does not locate) had a unique opportunity of photographing the "masks, statues, dance costumes and musical instruments," brought out from the hut where they were usually guarded, and set on the ground. His illustration shows a pair of these masks "peculiar to a sub-tribe [i.e., fraction] of the Senufo . . . the male carrying a quiver on his back," among a group of other, more familiar ritual objects. Since then only a comparatively few such masks have come to light; the best known are perhaps the pair in the Rietberg 80 Museum, first given their native name of déguélé by Holas in 1957.[61] 81

These really remarkable works were made in the Korhogo region only among the Kiembara, and in their ritual usage always appeared as a couple. Above a rather square-cut, adze-finished helmet with a large rectangular opening for the face, rises a figure with heavy legs whose body consists of only a series of bevelled rings for the male, and for the female of these rings and prominent breasts. The neck is again made of rings, carrying a large, strong head with the typical profile and thrusting mouth of the central region, topped by a headdress resembling a cock's comb. The male figure carries an empty quiver slung at his back, but neither figure has any arms. The whole is an extraordinary combination of geometric abstraction and expressively stylized naturalism.

It is clear that such a conception must embody considerable symbolic iconography. Holas informs us that *déguélé* is the vulgar name of this mask (which is restricted to the Fodombélé group), and that it probably has an unrevealed secret appellation, known only to the initiated. It appears only at night, when all the uninitiated are safely 15 in their houses, since to them its sight might possibly be fatal. In this it is unlike the more accessible rhythm pounder, the déblé, which can appear at any time and in the hands of the young initiates, while the use of the déguélé is restricted to the senior dignitaries of the lô society, even though both are employed in the same ceremonies: the burial and commemorative rites of important members of the society. The power of the déguélé, which embodies an idea accessible only to the highly initiated few, Holas says, "lies in the number of its rings, each corresponding to a precise volume of supernatural energy."[62] The apparently empty quiver of the male is really full of poisoned arrows, which may symbolize the celestial power of lightning, and which he must then shoot by will power alone. But other than this, there is no further explanation for the absence of arms in both of the figures. The cock's comb on the head, more detailed in some examples than in others, refers, Leuzinger suggests, to the "sacred bird of souls," which in one form or another appears so often in Senufo sculpture. It is interesting to note that the depiction of feet seems to be entirely optional with the artist, and perhaps the absence of the arms may be explained in a similar way: having no importance for the meaning and function of the mask, they have simply been omitted. For we must always remember that such formulations, related primarily to the world of deceased ancestors, have little to do with ordinary modes of representation.

Rhythm Pounders: Déblé

One of the finest of Senufo works (and indeed of African sculpture generally) is a tall female figure with short, spindle legs and feet 85 apparently sunk in a heavy cylindrical base, now in the collection of Madame Helena Rubinstein in Paris. The flow of its slender limbs and torso, the curved silhouette repeated in chin, breasts, belly and forearms, the limpid contraction and swelling of its parts and the rhythm of its spatial intervals—all these fuse into a striking unity. The dark surface of a smooth and polished patina is set off by bands of colored seeds and white cowries on the head, the chest, the arms and around the low waist. It is a work that crystallizes the image of a style.

This sculpture was brought back from the region of Sikasso (in the northern part of Senufo territory) by F.-H. Lem in 1935. When he published it in 1948 he described it as a "ritual female figure, supported on a heavy base. Borne by one of the participants, it is used to give rhythm to the evolutions of the dancers in the association of the Senufo-Pomporo, called "lô," which is a brotherhood of initiatory character."[63] This then is the first published example of a sculptural type now more generally known as the rhythm pounder.

The fact that we have its provenance is fortunate, for it enables us to localize a large number of the rhythm-pounders known to us today. 86 Lem himself collected another in the same region (now in the Chadourne collection), which by its differences as well as its similiarities allows us to see that we have here a style as well as a functional category of religious object.[64] The Chadourne figure is more upright and angular, the median line of breast and belly is sharper, the breasts and neck are thicker, the face somewhat flatter and the teeth more prominent. Yet it is clear from the general proportions, as well as from the handling of such details as the hair-crest, the ears and the hands, that these two figures are individual variations of a common regional style.

The other works of this style are undocumented, but comparison makes it evident that they come from the same region. The pounder 87 in the Schindler collection (which still retains its contrasting cowries) 88 and that belonging to Warner Muensterberger have very similar treatments of the breasts and shoulder, the same hollowed profile of the pointed belly and flat positioning of the fingers. The carving of the ear as a sunken disk flat to the side of the head, found on the Rubinstein 89 figure, is again present here, and also in two others (Verité and Ward- 90 well) of the same general style. These last, however, have somewhat different proportions, thinner arms, and a single sweeping convex (rather than concave) curve from beneath the breasts down to the navel. Although surely from the northern region, these two works are more like each other than they are like the rest of the group.

There is a pair of pounders in the Durand collection which is docu- 91 mented as having been brought from the far north—the region of San, the area where the Minianka live.[65] Although they are very weathered, and appear more attentuated than they once were, it is evident that as conceived they were taller and slenderer than the works in the Sikasso style. The heads are smaller, the necks, legs and bases are longer; the jaw curves further forward, and the simplified ears stand out at right angles to the head. The tendency to pare down, to treat forms sparingly and with a geometric emphasis, appears again in a 92 pounder (Ratton collection) which also has long legs and neck, and the same projecting ears, although this treatment of the buttocks is unique.[66] The body seems definitely northern, and has a flavor of Sudanese style as pronounced as in the San pair, and stronger than in the Sikasso group. Only the face, naturalistic and heart-shaped, the fuller breasts, and the careful scarifications suggest the possibility of connections with a more southerly style.

A pair of pounders in The Museum of Primitive Art presents allied 93 problems of style. Although elongated, like the northern examples, there is a squareness in the modelling (e.g., of the shoulders and the forearms), and an angularity in the joints very different from the fluid elliptical forms of the Sikasso group, and a vigor and solidity unlike the lightness of the San style, with which, once again, the faces do share certain traits.

One difficulty is the dearth of examples from the central region by which to define the style. The only documented ones are three collected by Storrer in 1954 in Lataha village, Korhogo district, among the 94 Kiembara fraction of the Senufo, two of which (now in the Rietberg 95 Museum and The Museum of Primitive Art) were a functional pair.[67] Although these two figures are considerably weathered by a stay in the open in one of the sacred groves, and each has some portions of the limbs missing, it is clear enough that this is a more naturalistic style, with less of the abstract rhythm of the Sikasso figures, and a much more organic expressiveness of bodily pose and facial expression. The formal simplifications here, just as successful in organizing the parts, spring less from concept and more from observation. Where the northern works are highly subtle, but impersonal monuments, here the thrust of the head against the neck, the weight of the body expressed in the elbows and the knees result in an effect of personal, subjective feeling.

Although Lem had given a summary indication of the function of these figures with heavy bases as rhythm pounders, it was Holas who, in 1957, first provided a detailed description of their use and meaning. His investigations were localized in the Korhogo region, where he was admitted to the rituals of the lô, and he illustrated his findings with the Rietberg Museum pounder.

Holas informs us that although these statues are known to the Senufo by "the vague and apocryphal name of katyéléo (the appellation Ka-Tyéléo being that of the great goddess who presides at initiation ceremonies)," and that although certain fractions give them "the common name of kpondo-sion, . . . whose approximate meaning is 'man of the sacred forest,' the name déblé, which is the only true name of the statue, is reserved for the exclusive usage of poro initiates."[68]

The arms of the figure, and the base, are its "functional parts," since during the commemorative rites the young initiates, in file, hold these statues by the arms and pound the earth in a slow rhythm. This act has a double meaning: "on the one hand the dull sound thus produced purifies the impure earth and renders it fertile and useful to humans; on the other it is an appeal to the souls of deceased ancestors, an invitation to them to participate, forcefully, in the religious ceremony."[69]

The rhythmic processions of the déblé are accompanied by the sounds of drums, gourd rattles, and a heavy wooden trumpet (néguel) which amplifies the words of the funeral chants, recited in the secret language of the lô society. The déblé makes four such appearances: on the evening of death when the procession comes from the sinzanga and visits the house of the deceased; during the actual burial; at the closing rites on the following night; and finally, during those ceremonies which are necessary for the proper separation of the dead from the living, when the déblé participate at the request of the survivors, who must pay a fee for this service and also provide the required sacrificial animals. For the Senufo "all these efforts are ritually indispensable, and any negligence or omission could provoke the anger of the spirit-world, with consequences fatal to the whole group."[70]

Holas adds that although the déblé is very often thus employed, it is not in origin, nor exclusively, devoted to the cult of the dead, but rather simply at its disposal when needed. And Himmelheber has noted that it also makes an appearance at the time of the tilling of the fields, in order to make them fertile.[71]

It is then, the déblé's ceremonial context, inseparable from its meaning, that also provides the minimum conditions of its form: it must have a heavy base (instead of feet), broad shoulders, and wide armpits. But these are conditions only; they hardly "explain" the care, the detail, the subtlety, and the individual variations with which these "functional" objects have been fashioned. In the result, these, too, are constituents of the meaning of the déblé.

Figures

The most numerous, and to the outside world the most familiar, of Senufo wooden sculptures is a female figure, standing, or less frequently sitting, and usually between six inches and two feet high. Both functionally and stylistically these works are part of a more heterogeneous group that includes representations of mother and child, standing male and equestrian figures, and more rarely seated or standing couples. Such sculptures are made in all parts of Senufo country; the role they play in the religious pantheon is everywhere the same and the formal variations they exhibit have more to do with region than with their meaning, type or pose. 96 97 98

The standing figures are ancestral representations; but since mythical, i.e., tribal, ancestors of the distant past, and the more recent real ancestors are shown in exactly the same way, once they are out of their ceremonial context there is no way of telling them apart. Maesen points out that the mythical ancestors are generally male, while the real ancestors, who are directly associated with fertility, are usually conceived in pairs; but individual figures are also made, and the fact that most of these are female may account for their preponderance in collections outside Africa. The ancestors, who play a benevolent, protective role, and of whom the Senufo are not at all afraid, are paid their respects by the collective community, with the village headman leading the ceremony.[72] Moreover, sculptural representations are not required for such rites, since any portion of the ancestor's earthly possessions may serve as an intermediary focus of communication. When, however, a figure is made, it is executed only after consultation with a member of the sandogo divinatory society.

This connection points up the further fact that many of these sculptures are used as divination instruments. The equestrian figures and the joined pairs especially have this purpose, and others as well, witness the pair brought back by Lem from Kenedougou, now in the 99

16 Sandogo society members carrying a figure. Central region, Naffara fraction. Photo: P. Knops, s.m.a., 1935

17 Women of the sandogo society dancing around the figure. Central region, Naffara fraction. Photo: P. Knops, s.m.a., 1935

Helena Rubinstein collection.[73] But such distinctions are not at all clear cut, and their attempted delineation may well be mistaken. One and the same object may have several functions simultaneously, and an ancestor figure can also serve as a fertility figure and a protective spirit which in turn may have a divinatory use.

One distinction can, however, be made. Besides the human representations in wood, there are also metal figures. They are small, often
175 grotesque in appearance with exaggerated facial features, enlarged
176 hands and feet, and a rough surface left unworked after casting. These are never real ancestor figures, but instead represent wandering ghosts who are hostile to humans and who must be placated so fre-
177 quently that the ancestors are often neglected. Small, hairy, pygmy-like beings, the ghosts beset human beings, mainly through women, who have organized in a society, the sandogo, which alone knows how to master them.[74] Sacrifices are imposed on the rest of the population, while the sandogo employs the figures as an essential part of its divination procedures. The ghost figures should also be distinguished from other technically similar metal castings of small animals (snake, turtle, chameleon, etc.) which women and children wear on a string around the waist or wrist, and men on the thumb, and which, like the wooden figures, are put into small shrines on the outside of the houses. These little metal figures, worn for protection, Maesen records, represent either mythical ancestors (yirigefolo), or totem animals (yawige), which are venerated as ancestors.[75] Once again, their purport and significance fuses, so that it is impossible to tell them apart.

Altogether there is thus a veritable host of minor entities whose function is to mediate between man and the invisible. It is, however, characteristic that in one way or another, directly and indirectly, they
16 are connected with the sandogo. Father Knops in 1934, documented an occasion when the sandogo was consulted on a course of action and, since the matter was of some importance, brought out a large figure supporting a cup. One of the women carried it on her head into
17 the village square, where the whole group danced around it while emitting a kind of gurgling chant. It was then placed in their midst

on the ground.[76] After the ceremony it was put back in its shrine, where it could be consulted privately. The sandogo society of each village, or of each of the larger village quarters, has a divinatory figure of this kind.

The over-all similarities of these figures, already mentioned, make it difficult to give an analytic canvass of specific style areas. Some characteristics of the various regions and their differences can nevertheless be noted. A standing figure collected in 1939, now in the collection of Dr. John Foley, is typical of the style of the central region. 109 In profile there is the repetitive forward thrust of coiffure, jaw, breasts, belly, knees and feet against the strong axis of the back, a manner of composition which is to be found, with variations, in other areas as well. More particular to the central region is the sense of slenderness that goes with these thrusting forms, and that is especially evident in the upper arms from which the rings of ornamental bracelets stand out. Characteristic, too, is the elliptically outlined headdress, finishing at the front with an upward reverse twist. The face of this figure, however, is more convex than most, other works from this region having scooped out cheeks that join the slightly convex chin line to produce a thin, slightly open mouth. The style is again well illustrated by the pair of small figures brought back by Lem from Korhogo.[77] These features are found in works of different kinds, whether the standing figures (The Museum of Primitive Art) or the seated 110 (Hirsch), or those that are attached to useful objects (Himmelheber 100 and Anspach); even those that are somewhat stockier in their proportions are evidently variations on this same style. 103 104

A seated figure now in the collection of Professor Vandenhoute, collected by Maesen in 1939 at Dembasso among the Niéné fraction, 105 may perhaps serve as the prototype of the western style. In many ways similar to the works just considered, the taut fusion of elongation and bulge is less marked, the lips of the open mouth are more independent of the chin, and the forward portion of the headdress now sweeps down over the nose. A standing figure in the Buffalo Museum 106 exhibits all the characteristics in a more pronounced fashion, and is presumably from the same western area near Kolia. With this area, too, must be associated a number of much larger figures of a seated mother with child only recently brought out from, we are told, the area of Boundiali. They are exceptional not only for their size (between 107 3 and 4 feet), but also for the angular simplification of their carving which results in cylindrical limbs and 90° elbow joints, and the elaboration of a heavy coiffure with pendants on the sides and in front. A group of a mother nursing two children in the Abidjan Museum has 108 these same characteristics, and the same vigorous, somewhat coarse expression in the face, and so must be closely related in style. Altogether, the group exhibits many signs of untraditional carving.

Due to the accidents of collecting, the style of the northern region has been best documented, both in the number of figures and the record of the date when they were found. Three pieces of very similar style can be traced back at least to the middle 'thirties. One was collected at Bobo-Dioulasso by Kjersmeier, who calls it a Bobo divination figure; another was found at Sikasso by Lem who groups it with the Senufo but considers it of Bambara origin, and a third was in the collection of Tristan Tzara well before 1935. A fourth figure, whose 115 European history must be at least as long, now in the Webster Plass Collection of the British Museum, was formerly in the possession of Felix Fénéon who called it Senufo-Toussia.[78] These works have in common a certain squareness of face and shoulders, pointed breasts and short legs, and especially a conical belly on which the radiating lines of the sun-fertility motif has been inscribed in large scale, all of which are found again in a work in the Hersey collection. Almost surely related is a remarkable and monumental small figure in the Wielgus 118 collection, whose lower portion has been mutilated by fire. The extreme, and effective, stylization of the head is found again in other works (notably two equestrian figures, one topping a helmet mask—Merkel and Cohen collections) whose body treatment is like that of 119 the northern rhythm pounders. 77

From the same northern region come two other figures also long in the Kjersmeier collection characterized by a blocked out quality in the modelling, which reduces both face and figure to a minimum number of simple planes and omits almost all detail.[79] The resultant style, less refined but perhaps stronger than the small figures from the Korhogo area, can be seen again in an example in the Musée de 121 l'Homme which is undocumented but clearly must come from this same region.

There is still another group of figures that can be associated with the north. It also includes works whose exact provenance is unknown, but which have been in European collections for many years: two belonged to Albert Barnes by at least 1926; two others (then in the Derain and Carré collections) were included in The Museum of Modern 122 Art exhibition of 1935.[80] On the analogy of the rhythm pounders, whose 123 simplified elongated body and ovoid head with scooped-out face these figures also exhibit, they probably stem from the Sikasso region. In fact, the figure formerly in the possession of André Derain, like another one in the Arnold Newman collection, has been broken at the 127 legs, and is even so nearly three feet tall; it is possible that both ended in heavy bases and were carved as rhythm pounders.

18 Initiant with ring of silence. Central region, Korhogo district, Kiembara fraction. Photo: Emil Storrer

Daleu

In form the téfolopitian, or daleu, is a long slender staff topped by a small figure. Carved in wood, or cast in metal, this figure, usually a 128 seated female, closely resembles in style the somewhat larger ancestral and divinatory representations.[81] The daleu has been described as a trophy figure, an agricultural staff, and an initiation prize.

It seems to function chiefly as an award or "diploma" presented to winners of an agricultural competition among members of the young peoples age-grade groupings. These events take place when, because the village must break ground for new fields, there is an extra and heavy load of work, and they thus have an immediate practical purpose. The daleu is given to the most skillful tiller of the soil in his group; he carries his trophy back from the fields to the sound of the big lô drums, and he may keep it in his hut until the next such occasion, when it will be used again in the same way.[82] But it is more than a pragmatic social object. The festival in which it appears is related to the homage that must be paid to certain earth spirits, and has its parallel among the Bambara. There the young men of the flan tyé kuru hold hoeing contests with those of neighboring villages and the winners are allowed to dance with the antelope headdresses, or tji wara. Like the Bambara antelope, the Senufo daleu is thus symbolic of fertility.[83] It is also related to the lô, since the young competitors are society initiates, members of the lô age-grades, and the competition has a ceremonial character. The daleu is besides connected with the lô in other ways. In some regions it is awarded to initiates for mastery of the secret language of the lô, and it serves at 8 promotion ceremonies. Among the Kiembara—as Bochet's drawing shows—it is held by the kpélié-masked dancer, while among other fractions it "is considered a weapon of Kâtiéléo [earth mother] used to repulse any harmful influences which might, with results dangerous to those participating, alter the course of the religious ceremonies."[84] It can therefore be seen that the somewhat variable and manifold uses of the daleu figure (which sometimes appears without its staff) are generally connected with fertility.

There are other sculptures given, like the daleu, as prizes in these same agricultural ceremonies. They are images of birds, mounted on the ends of poles, or perches, and shown in flight.[85] Sometimes also 168 called dance standards, they are made in both wood and, somewhat smaller, in metal. They may be single figures, or groups in which 137 smaller birds (representing hawks) are made to hover above the out- 138 stretched wings of the larger one (representing a vulture), by means of small rods. One such group, collected by Lem in the Kenedougou area, even includes a female figure standing on the back of the larger bird.[86]

Rings of Silence: Nyi-kar-yi

As has already been noted, during the time the short-lived Massa cult of 1952-53 supplanted the older religious customs, it brought to light a number of traditional works of art that had hitherto been carefully guarded. Among them was a group of small bronze rings decorated with a bovine head and horns, known as rings of silence, 139 or by their native name of nyi-kar-yi. Father Clamens was the first (in 1953) to publish a group of these rings, which he had collected among the Kiembara fraction in the Korhogo district, and especially in the village of Watyene.[87] The rings were employed as part of the ceremonies initiating young men into the lô society. As each candidate, after completing his necessary period of endurance in the bush, was sworn in by the officiating elders, endowed with his new, secret name and told the password, he was also given a ring, which he at once put on his thumb. Then the new members returned to the village, 18 dressed as our illustration shows, with knitted cap, cowrie bracelets, necklace, and loin cloth, and carrying bow, arrows and snuff. The ring was now held in the mouth, and with their silence thus ensured they

19 Fetish figure (kafiguélédio). Central region, Korhogo district. Wood, cloth, feathers, fibre, bone, iron, 32″ high. MPA 64.3 Gift of Mr. and Mrs. Raymond Wielgus

20 X-ray photograph of fetish figure (kafiguélédio)

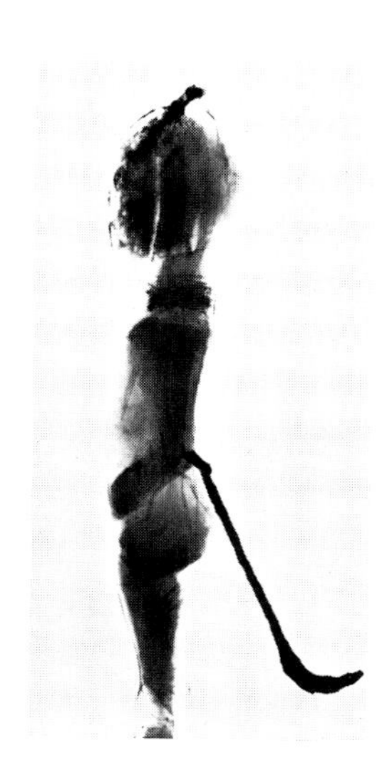

paid their respects to the elders of the society, sitting in front of the doors to their houses, offering each one in turn a pinch of snuff. In this fashion the young men enacted for all to see a ritual symbolizing the silence they must henceforth observe concerning the secret knowledge and practices of the lô society, of which they were now accepted members. Our illustration shows one of the Naffara initiates wearing 18 a ring of somewhat different shape and construction than those found by Father Clamens (since they vary from place to place), but serving the same ritual purpose. At the close of the ceremony the young men return to the grove, where they deposit the rings, to be used the following year by a new group of novitiates.

Fetish Figures: Kafiguélédio

The Massa cult of the early 'fifties also brought to light a type of figure which, possessing magic powers within itself, may properly be called a fetish. This is the kafiguélédio, found, so far as one knows, only 142 among certain fractions inhabiting the central region.[88] Although it is in one sense only on the borderline of sculpture, it is—even outside its original sanctuary setting—a very effective and disturbing presence. At its core is a very roughly carved wooden figure, but this shows 19 only at the feet. The rest is covered with an unfinished burlap draped 20 loosely over the body, drawn together by a cord at the neck, and then flaring out toward the top of the head in an inverted triangle crowned with feathers and porcupine quills. Tied on to the moveable arms are wood or metal weapons. The one in the right hand usually being curved or bent. The cloth is often stiff with a dried and darkened coating of sacrificial animal blood and eggs, while rams or antelope horns, and little wrapped bundles, all filled with magic substances, attached to the figure, add to its magic power. "Given our scanty information on the ritual usage of the kafiguélédio, one may suppose that in the course of a secret geomantic session the operator 'threw' the evil spell by pointing the arms of the statuette in the direction of the individual at whom it was aimed."[89] Here is one of the rare instances in which one may properly talk of black magic practices.

The Hornbill: Sétien

Among the most pervasive representations in the repertory of Senufo sculpture is a bird with a small round head bare of plumage, a long beak, prominent belly and spread, rectangular wings that stands in the suggestion of a human pose. As we have already seen, it appears as a "totemic" crest on the top of many face masks, and is placed between the horns of animal helmet masks; it decorates the covers of ointment boxes and is carved in relief on the sculptured doors. This bird is the hornbill, or sétien. According to Senufo belief, the sétien—along with chameleon, the tortoise, the serpent and the crocodile, also shown frequently—was one of the first five living creatures, and was the first to be killed for food.[90] In its allegoric form, with its long beak touching, or almost touching, its swollen belly to suggest the male and female components of increase, it is called porpianong or porparga. This means, says Holas, that it stands for the whole category of the porpia, tribal effigies symbolizing the continuity of the whole community, or "the constituent elements of the collectivity."[91]

Small renderings of the hornbill, either in combination, as on the masks and doors, or separately, have been known for a long time.[92] However, in the last few years very large sculptures of this bird standing four feet or more high on a flat or rounded base have appeared in considerable numbers. Proportions and stance vary, but there is always the essential emphasis on beak and belly; although most are bareheaded, some carry a cock's crest. Many are painted with triangles, lozenges, or spots in red and white, suggesting plumage, but it does not appear that all of those that lack color have lost it through weathering. A snake often climbs up the middle of the back, and some examples carry their own small progeny perched on their outspread wings as additional symbols of fecundity. Despite these style variations (some of which are undoubtedly due to very recent production), to the best of our knowledge all the birds of this scale come from the central Senufo region. This, at any rate, is what is indicated by the very rare and imprecise documentation.

146 145 147

These large birds play their own part in the ceremonies of the lô society, when, heavy as they are, they are carried on the heads of members taking part in the rituals, symbols of the living forces of the universe. This explains why the base of many of these sculptures is hollowed out underneath, so that it may fit like a cap on the head of the wearer and thus help to steady its weight. (There is also a sculptured group showing a seated woman who holds up such a bird.) But it should be noted that many of the birds stand on cylindrical bases that have never been hollowed out and seem designed to rest upon the ground. This points to a different, even if possibly an allied, ceremonial usage.[93]

150 149 148

Pulley Holders

Pulley holders have long been among the best known and most popular of African sculptural forms. Functionally, they are simply mechanical artifacts, serving the same purpose among the Baule, the Guro, the Dogon, the Bambara or the Senufo: a device which, suspended over the loom holds a pulley over which, on turn, passes a cord that raises and lowers the heddle controlling the warp threads so that the weaving shuttle may be threaded between them. The sculptural elaboration given to the pulley has thus nothing to do with its practical working, and although the miniature head, or the mask, or the occasional complete figure which decorates it may provide some supervisory protection (in most cases by conventional association), it is very largely gratuitous—except to the esthetic sense.[94] Thus in its appreciation as an individual object separated from its context the pulley holder suffers less from museological diffraction than the ritual mask or figure.

152

The motifs that crown the pulley holders run the gamut of the larger, ceremonially important sculptures: face masks and animals masks that vary in type and style with the region, and, most common, the bird's head or a fusion of bird beak and human features. All these are treated with considerable plastic freedom and invention, and all degrees of naturalism and stylization can be found. Since the pulley holder must be hung, either from a tree or from a frame above the loom, a long beak, or an elongated countenance is a favored motif, because apart from its associations, it allows the suspension cord to pass beneath the neck of the sculpture with little danger of its slipping off, and does away with the need for the loop hole cut out at the top of other representations. Given the range of the major forms of Senufo sculpture, it is not surprising that their pulley holders should have a greater variety than those of their neighbors.

Relief Sculpture

For many technical and ritual reasons, relief sculpture plays a lesser role than sculpture in the round. As among the Baule, and the Bambara and the Dogon, it decorates drums and the doors of houses (although not of granaries as in the north). Most of the doors belong to the secret-society shrines built within the sacred groves, where ritual statues and masks, costumes and dance paraphernalia are housed when not in use; others, however, served as social insignia (status symbols) of the rich and powerful families of the village, or the important houses sheltering the traditional treasures of the oldest chiefdom.

Wherever the doors were used, their decoration and symbolism is very much the same. The main motif is a large, rectangular panel 157 having a hollow disk at its center, and divided into four triangular or elliptical fields by lines radiating from the center to the corners. The disk is a symbol for the sun, and sometimes is decorated with a relief carving of a spider, which is itself a solar motif. The four fields contain incised geometric patterns (within which figures may occur) that also are symbolic: crescents indicating the moon, triangles meaning mountains and ellipses streams, while over-all crosshatchings are said to refer to fields with crops.[95]

The relief in the two bands above and below commonly show the familiar animal emblems of fertility: snake and crocodile, turtle, frog, chameleon and hornbill, as well as an occasional antelope and lizard. 158 This is apparently also the meaning of those groups in which one animal eats another, or there is a mutual devouring. A popular motif is a human figure shown standing or riding, with guns or knives, or guarding a file of prisoners (whose manacles are sometimes a separate motif), and a representation of the face mask is often given prominence. Everything represented, then, has some sort of meaningful and familiar reference; but these indications are apparently not linked in any larger iconographical program, and in this sense the sculptured reliefs serve principally as (understandable) decoration.

All of these doors originally had a lock of the type, Arabic in origin, that is common throughout the whole region of the southern Sudan. Identical in mechanism, they are all very much alike in style, and that style is not Senufo. There are, of course, examples with unmistakable Dogon or Bambara features—heads or figures. But most locks simply have a very generalized Sudanese appearance, given by geometrical incisions, which, where it can be localized at all bears some resemblance to Bambara conventions of linear pattern and a face topped with a leaf-shaped or flame-like headdress. It is remarkable that the design 158 of the door never takes into account the eventual addition of the lock, which is simply applied to it and so disturbs its symmetrical pattern. All this points to the fact that among the Senufo the lock is a standard device imported from the north (perhaps from the Malinké) and sold to the Senufo by the Mandé traders.

Since we have scanty information concerning exact provenances, and since most doors follow the same general decorative scheme, which allows latitude in the details, it is difficult to determine if there are any true regional styles. The door now in the collection of Mrs. Frans Olbrechts, collected by Maesen in 1939, but made as early as 157 1925 by Yalokone in Boundiali, is probably typical for that area.[96] Its distinguishing characteristic is the insertion of figures on the hatched fields of the central panel, a feature repeated in the well-known example belonging to the University Museum (collected before 1930) and in a door in the Verheyleweghen collection.[97] But this motif is present 158 in a rougher, less precisely finished form on many other examples (e.g., that belonging to Mrs. Eugene Meyer, which also dates from before 1930) and so may well have been common to the whole central 159 area.[98] In contrast, those designs which limit the middle panel to a purely geometric ornament probably come only from the north. The 161 design—in tiers and without any panel—of the door from the Korhogo district in the Musée de l'Homme is altogether exceptional. 162

The repertory of decorative-mythological motifs is almost identical in all relief sculptures. It occurs on the body of the ritual drums, and on the sculptured wooden receptacles that support the two kinds of "fetishes" (the tièbè and the tendrigi) described by Father Clamens as part of an important cult of the Korhogo region. These supports, which are all alike in having four short legs, are as a class called pliéwo, or pliwoho (black night), a name which has then been applied to the drum itself.[99] As Maesen had already pointed out, the legs (some 164 of which have bent knees and rudimentary feet) stand for human legs, since young girls carry the drums on their heads. The drums may be put on the ground in front of a hut only on the occasion of a burial or memorial ritual, and then must not be touched. This supporting pose is shown by the figures carved around the circumference of one of the tendrigi illustrated by Father Clamens, while in the Ratton collec- 165 tion there is a drum held up by a seated female figure who replaces the usual legs. The legs then are symbolic substitutes for the human support the drum should have during ceremonial usage. All this is evident in the drum (collected by Maesen) now in the Antwerp Ethnographic Museum said to have been made in 1904. Like the others, it 163 is covered with an animal hide, whose fringe and fastening mechanism, including pegs and binding ring, are shown carved in wood just below the actual hide. From bottom to top it thus contains three different kinds of decorative symbolism.

21

21 Dancer with face mask, 1954. Central region, Korhogo district, Lataha village, Kiembara fraction 22 Face mask (kpélié) with accoutrements. Central region, Korhogo district [S]. Wood, horn, fibre, cloth, feathers, aluminum, 14⅛″ high. MPA 64.10

22

23 24 25

23 Face mask (kpélié). Central region, Korhogo district [S]. Wood, 15″ high. Collection Mr. and Mrs. Arnold Newman, New York 24 Face mask (kpélié). Central region, Korhogo district [S]. Wood, 15¼″ high. MPA 61.183 25 Face mask (kpélié). Central region, Korhogo district [S]. Wood, 14¾″ high. Collection Mr. Joseph Floch, New York

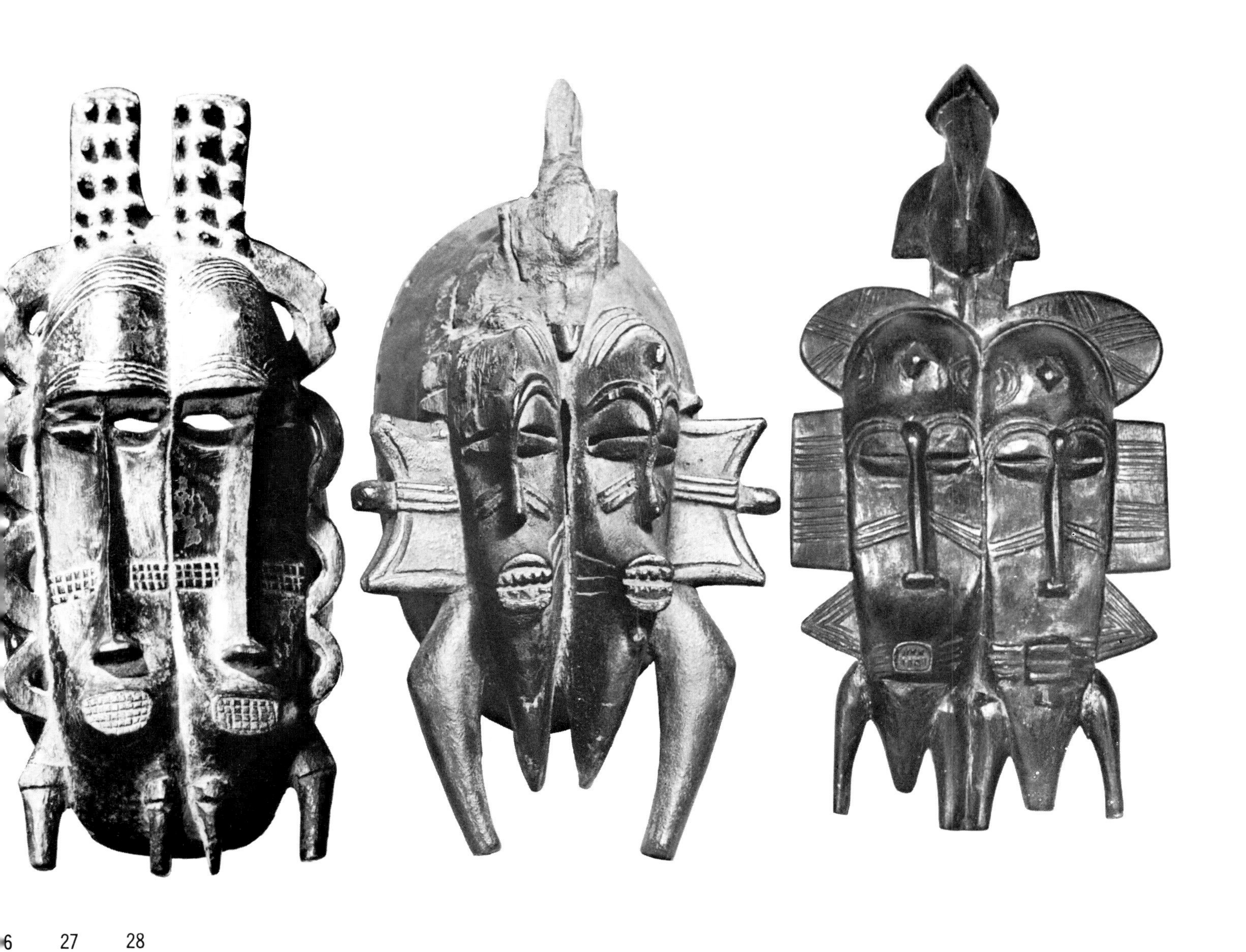

6 27 28

26 Double face mask (kpélié). Central region [S]. Wood, 9¾″ high. MPA 60.2 27 Double face mask (kpélié). Central region, Korhogo district [S]. Wood, 11¾″ high. Collection Mr. J. Païlès, Paris 28 Double face mask (kpélié). Central region [S]. Wood, 14¾″ high. Collection Mr. Mathias Komor, New York

29 30 31

29 Face mask (kpélié). Central region, Korhogo, Kiembara fraction [F: collected by Dr. Albert Maesen in 1938]. Wood, 13¾″ high. Etnografisch Museum, Antwerp AE.55.43.15 30 Face mask (kpélié). Central region, Korhogo district, Guiembé village, Kiembara fraction [F: collected by Mr. Emil Storrer]. Wood, 12½″ high. Rijksmuseum voor Volkenkunde, Leiden 2818-1 31 Face mask (kpélié). Central region, Korhogo district, Kokwo village, Kiembara fraction [F: collected by Dr. Albert Maesen in 1939]. Wood, 13$\frac{5}{16}$″ high. Collection Dr. Albert Maesen, St. Pieters-Woluwe, Belgium 32 Face mask (kpélié). Northern region [S: cf. Lem Pl.50]. Wood, 14¼″ high. Collection Dr. Hans Himmelheber, Heidelberg 33 Face mask (kpélié). Northern region [S: cf. Lem Pl.50]. Wood, 16″ high. MPA 59.293

32 33

34 35 36

34 Face mask (kpélié?). Southeastern region, Dabakala district, Djimini fraction [S]. Wood, traces of paint, 14" high. Collection Mr. and Mrs. Samuel Rubin, New York 35 Face mask (kpélié?). Southeastern region [S]. Wood, 15⅛" high. MPA 60.169 36 Face mask (kpélié?). Southeastern region [S]. Wood, traces of paint, 14" high. Collection Mr. Paul Tishman, New York

37 Face mask (kpélié?). Southeastern region [S]. Wood, tin, 13⅜" high. Collection Galerie Le Corneur-Roudillon, Paris 38 Face mask (kpélié?). Southeastern region [S]. Wood, metal, 15" high. Collection Mr. and Mrs. H. Barnet, New York

37 38

39 Face mask (kpélié). Central region, Korhogo district [S]. Copper, 11″ high. Rijksmuseum voor Volkenkunde, Leiden 3394-2 40 Face mask (kpélié). Central region, Korhogo district, Sinématiali village, Naffara fraction [F: collected by Father P. Knops in 1935]. Copper, 10¾″ high. Afrika-Centrum, Cadier en Keer, Holland AC 54.2.16 41 Face mask (kpélié). Central region, Korhogo district [A]. Bronze, 9⅞″ high. Collection Mr. and Mrs. Jean Verheyleweghen, Brussels 42 Face mask (kpélié). Central region [S]. Wood. Musée de l'Homme, Paris M.H. 21.4.17 43 Face mask (kpélié). Bronze, 10⅞″ high. MPA 59.294 44 Face mask (kpélié). Bronze, 8¼″ high. MPA 61.37

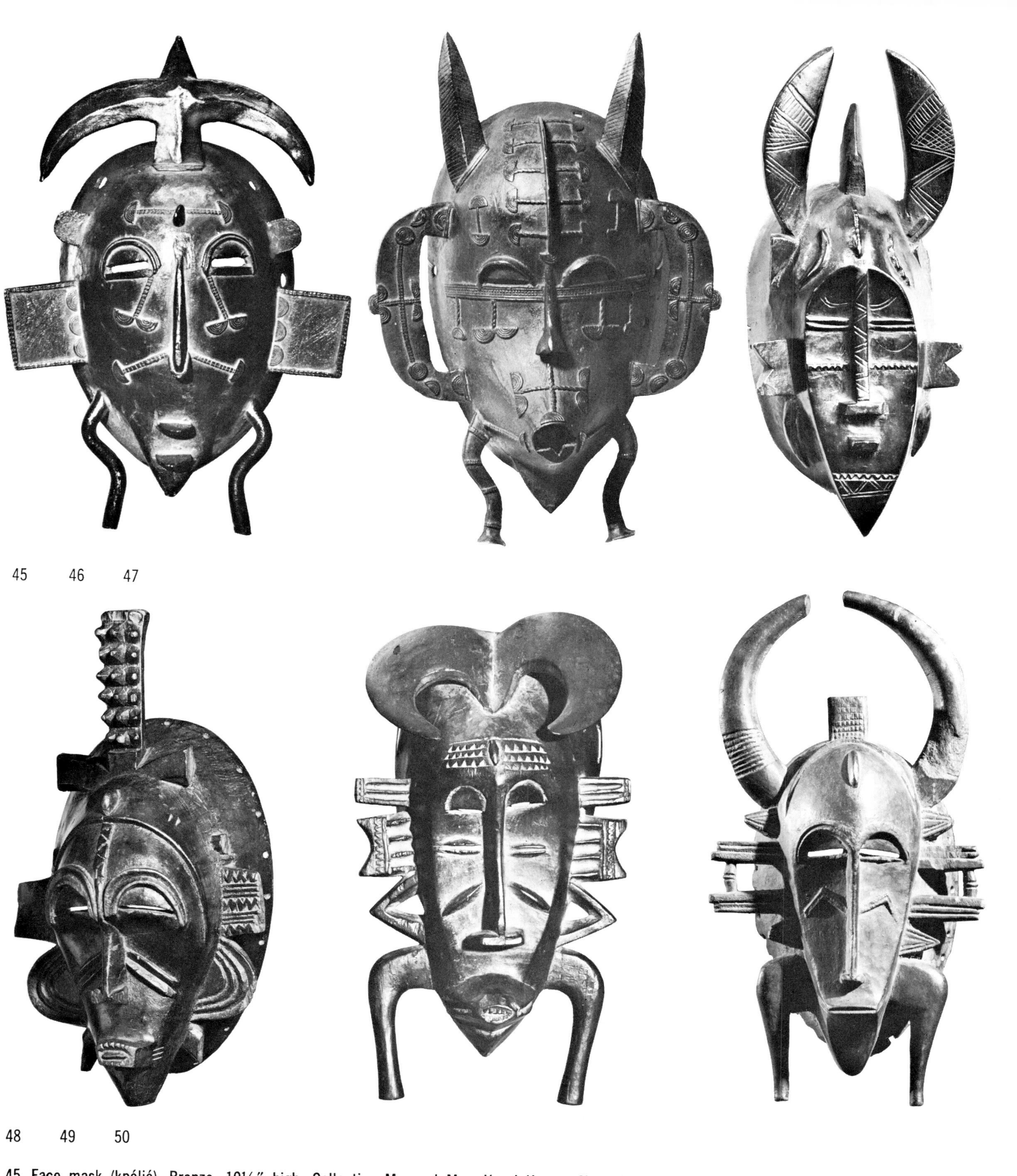

45 Face mask (kpélié). Bronze, 10¼″ high. Collection Mr. and Mrs. Henri Kamer, New York 46 Face mask (kpélié). Bronze, 10⅝″ high. Collection Mr. and Mrs. Jean Verheyleweghen, Brussels 47 Face mask (kpélié). Central region [S]. Wood, 11¾″ high. Collection Galerie Le Corneur-Roudillon, Paris 48 Face mask (kpélié). Central region [S]. Wood, 11″ high. Collection Dr. A. Corman, Tarbes, France 49 Face mask (kpélié). Central region [S]. Wood, 12″ high. Collection Mr. Ernst Anspach, New York 50 Face mask (kpélié). Central region [S]. Wood, 12½″ high. MPA 59.295

51 52

53

54

51 Helmet mask ("Firespitter"). Central region, Korhogo district [S]. Wood, 33½" high. Collection Mrs. Frans M. Olbrechts, Wezembeek, Belgium 52 Helmet mask ("Firespitter"). Central region, Korhogo district [S]. Wood, 36" long. Musée de l'Homme, Paris X50-368 53 Helmet mask ("Firespitter"). Central region [S]. Wood, 31½" long. Rijksmuseum voor Volkenkunde, Leiden 3319-6 54 Helmet mask ("Firespitter"). Central region [S]. Wood, 35⅝" long. MPA 57.248

55

55 Helmet mask. Central region [S]. Wood, 17¾" long. British Museum 1956 Af.27.40   56, 56a Helmet mask. Central region, Korhogo district, Faïdonga village. [F: collected by Mr. F.-H. Lem]. Wood, 17½" long. Collection Madame Helena Rubinstein, Paris

56

56a

58

59

57 Double helmet mask ("Firespitter") with costume. Central region, Nebunyonkaa village, Kiembara fraction [F: collected by Dr. Albert Maesen in 1939]. Wood, native cotton, paint, 29" long. Etnografisch Museum, Antwerp AE.55.30.23 58 Double helmet mask ("Firespitter"). Central region [S]. Wood, paint, 38" long. Collection Mr. Eliot Elisofon, New York 59 Double helmet mask ("Firespitter"). Central region, Korhogo district, Ladio-kaha village [F: collected by Mr. Emil Storrer in 1952]. Wood, traces of paint, 25½" long. MPA 57.266

60 Dancer with helmet mask in initiation ceremony, 1954. Central region, Korhogo district, Sinématiali village, Naffara fraction 61 Helmet mask with costume. Central region [S]. Wood, copper, fibre, 15¾" long. Rijksmuseum voor Volkenkunde, Leiden 3432-2

60

61

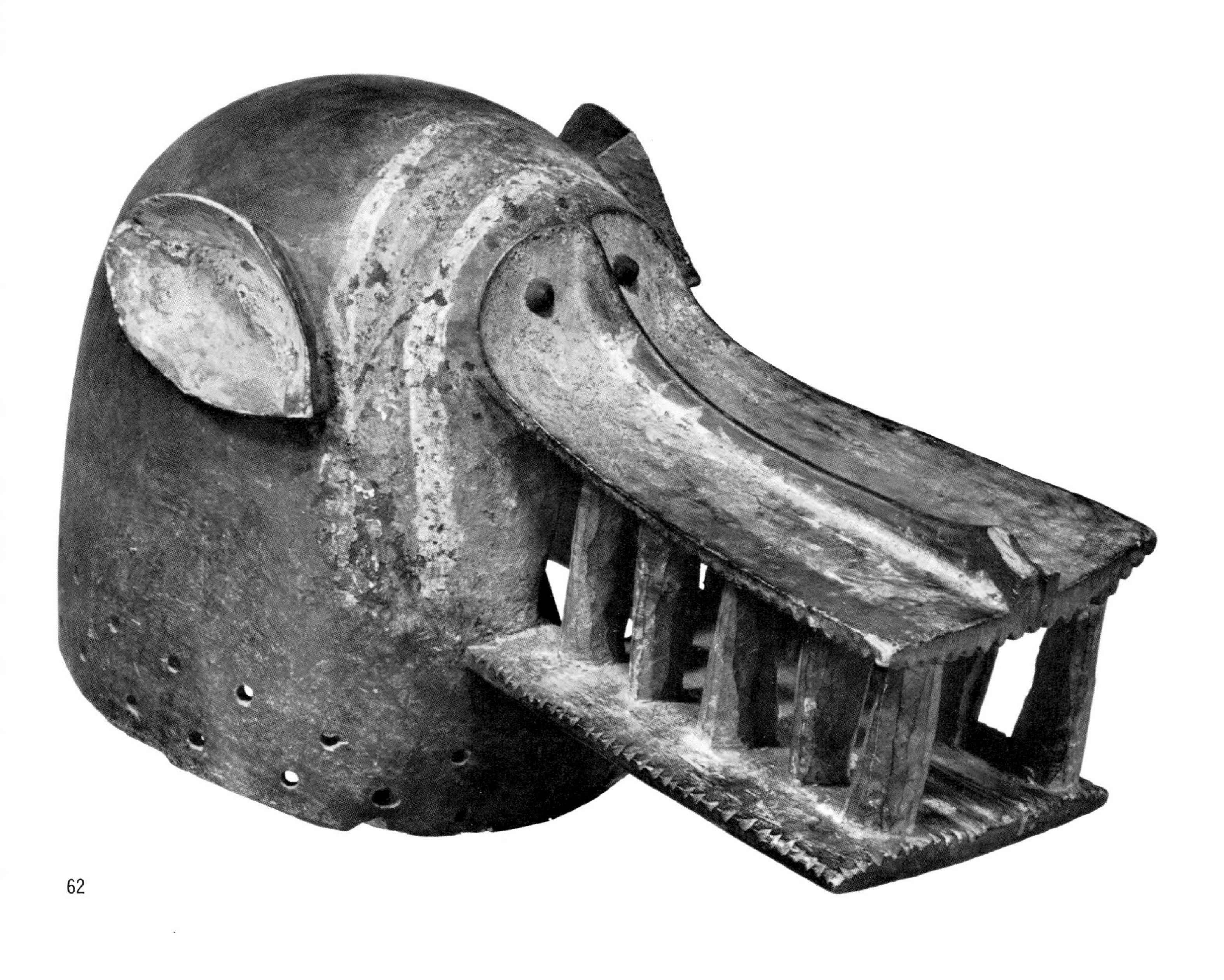

62

62 Helmet mask. Central region? [S]. Wood, traces of paint, 10″ long. Seattle Art Museum, Eugene Fuller Memorial Collection Af.16.4 63 Helmet mask. Northern region, Sikasso (Folona?) district, Siene village [F: collected by Mr. F.-H. Lem]. Wood, 22″ high. Collection Madame Helena Rubinstein, Paris 64 Helmet mask. Wood, traces of paint, 18⅛″ long. MPA 59.216 65 Helmet mask. Wood, 15½″ long. Collection Mr. and Mrs. Samuel Rubin, New York

3

4

5

66

67

66 Helmet mask. Northern region [A: cf. Elisofon Pl.109]. Wood, 27½″ high. MPA 56.373 67 Headdress. Northern region? [F: collected by Mr F.-H. Lem in Fenkolo village, Sikasso district]. Wood, metal repairs, 19½″ high. Collection Madame Helena Rubinstein, Paris 68, 68a Double helmet mask ("Firespitter"). Central region? [S]. Wood, 25″ long. Collection Mr. Donald Deskey, courtesy Peabody Museum of Archaeology and Ethnology, Harvard University

68

68a

69

70 71

72 73

74

69 Masked figures (nassolo) dancing in initiation ceremony, 1954. Central region, Korhogo district, Sinématiali village, Naffara fraction. (The carved animal head can be seen at the far end of the group.) 70 Mask. Central region, Ferkessédougou district, Naffara fraction [S]. Wood, 34″ long. Collection Dr. Jack V. Wallinga, St. Paul 71 Mask. Central region, Ferkessédougou district, Naffara fraction [S]. Wood, traces of paint, 34″ long. MPA 64.13. Gift of Mrs. Gertrud A. Mellon

72 Helmet mask. Wood, 16½″ high. American Museum of Natural History, New York 90.2-3447 73 Helmet mask. Wood, 11⅞″ high. MPA 59.6
74 Mask. Wood, encrustation, 23¾″ long. Collection Mr. and Mrs. Samuel Rubin, New York

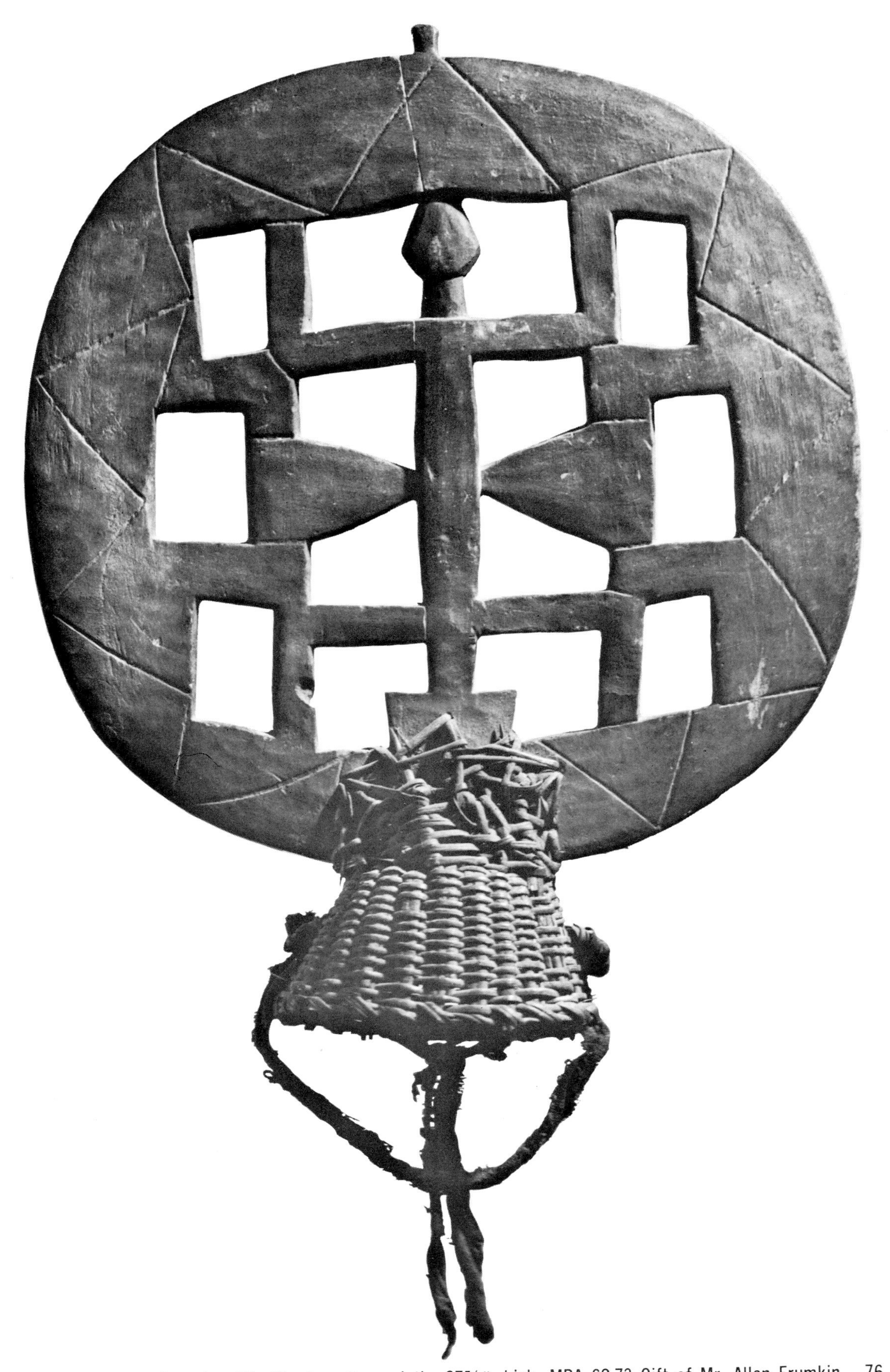

75

75 Headdress (kwonro). Central region [A]. Wood, rattan, cloth, 27⅝" high. MPA 62.73 Gift of Mr. Allan Frumkin 76 Crest of headdress (kwonro). Central region? [A]. Wood, 20½" high. Collection Mr. Georges de Menil, New York 77 Equestrian figure on helmet. Northern region [S]. Wood, 18" high. Collection Mr. and Mrs. Arthur A. Cohen, New York

76

77

78 79

79a

78 Headdress? Wood, 50⅝″ high, 22⅛″ wide. MPA 60.17 79, 79a Headdress? Wood, 51″ high, 24″ wide. Collection Mr. Aaron Furman, New York

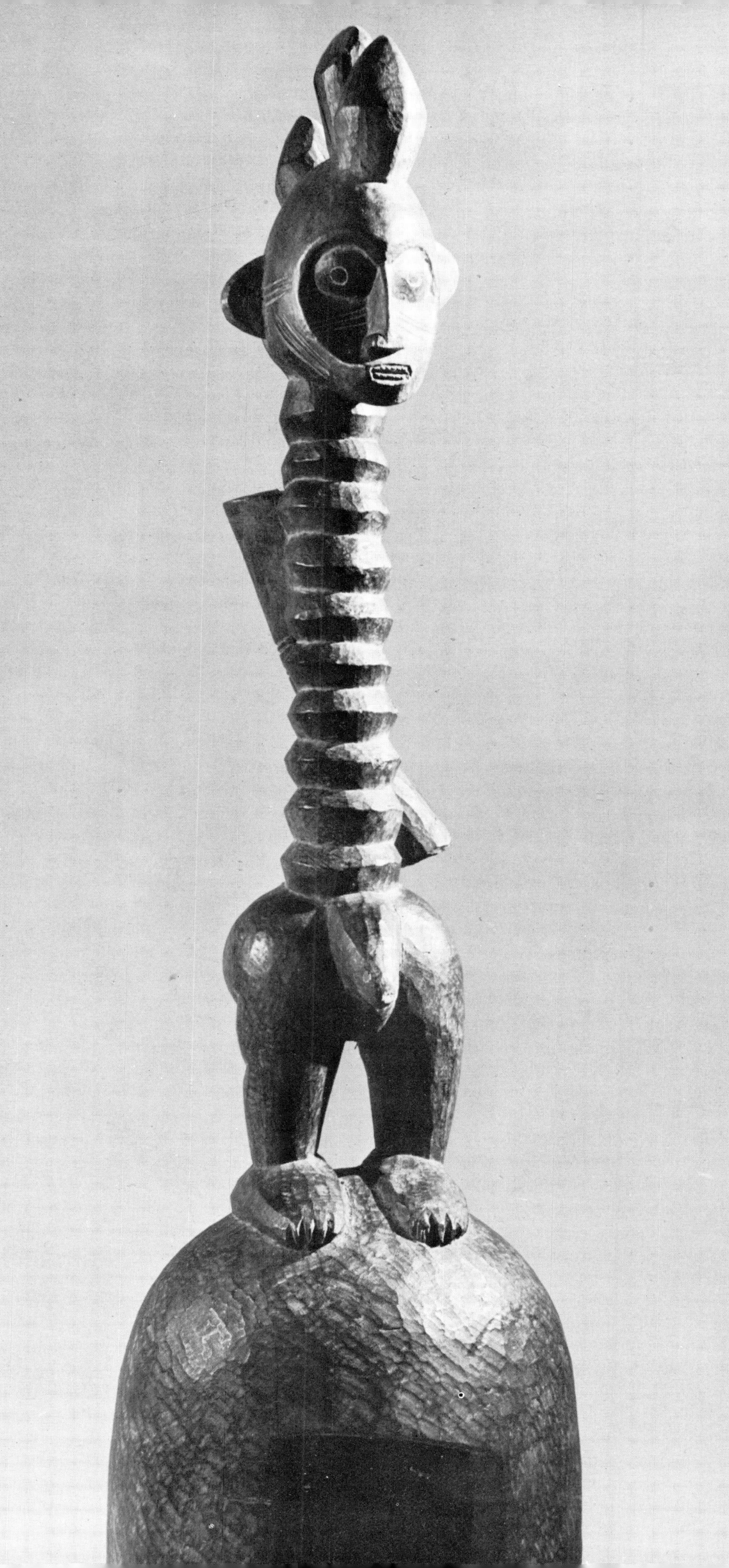

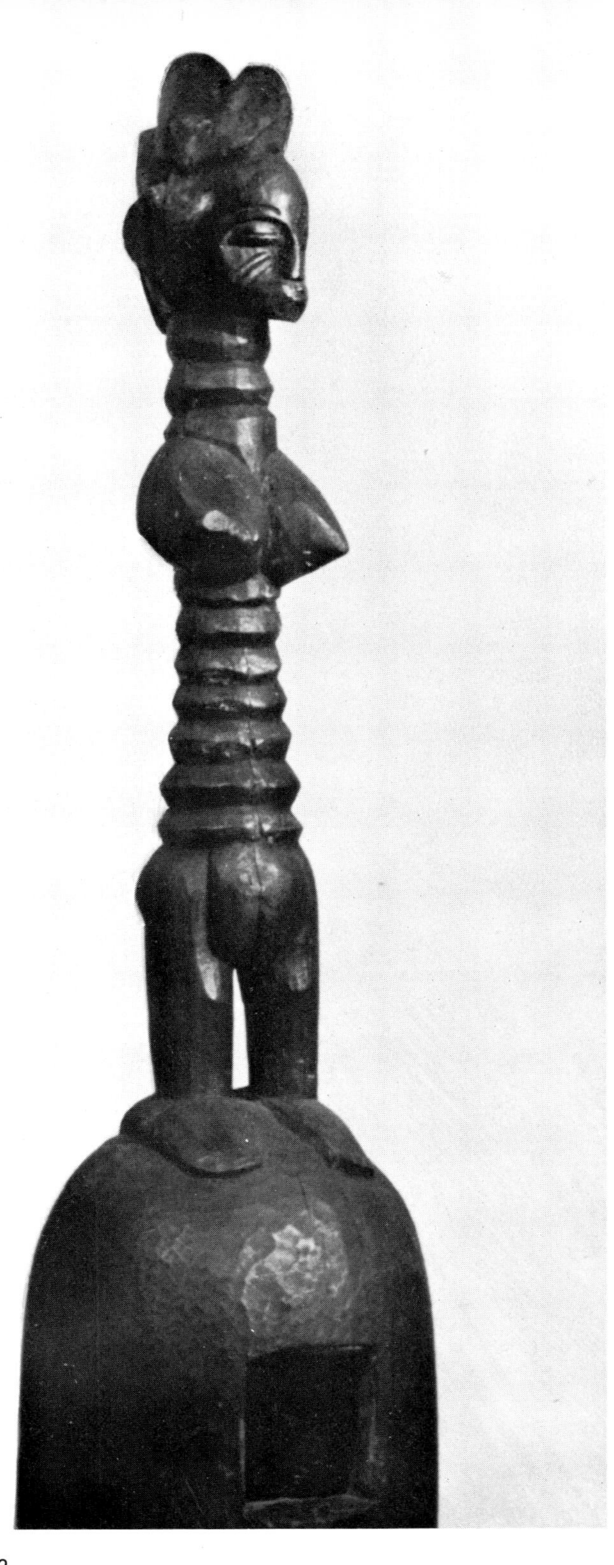

82 83

80, 81 Pair of helmet masks (déguélé). Central region, Korhogo district [A]. Female, wood, 36¼″ high; male, wood, 39″ high. Museum Rietberg, Zürich RAF 302 82 Helmet mask, female (déguélé). Central region, Korhogo district, Kokwo village, Kiembara fraction [F: collected by Dr. Albert Maesen in 1939]. Wood, 38¾″ high. Etnografisch Museum, Antwerp AE.55.37.29 83 Helmet mask, female (déguélé). Central region, Korhogo district [S: cf. no. 82]. Wood. 34¼″ high. Collection Dr. A. Corman, Tarbes, France 84 Pair of helmet masks (déguélé). Central region, Korhogo district [S: cf. no. 82]. Female, wood, 33⅜″ high; male, wood, 33¼″ high. Collection Mr. Eliot Elisofon, New York

85 85a

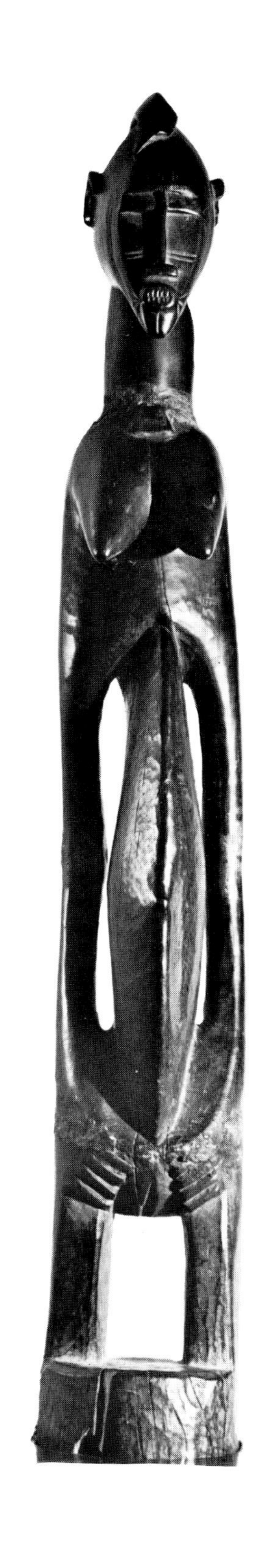

86 86a

85, 85a Rhythm pounder, female (déblé). Northern region, Sikasso district [F: collected by Mr. F.-H. Lem]. Wood, cowries, kisi seeds, 35¾″ high. Collection Madame Helena Rubinstein, Paris 86, 86a Rhythm pounder, female (déblé). Northern region, Sikasso district [F: collected by Mr. F.-H. Lem]. Wood, 38″ high. Collection Mr. Paul Chadourne, Garches, France

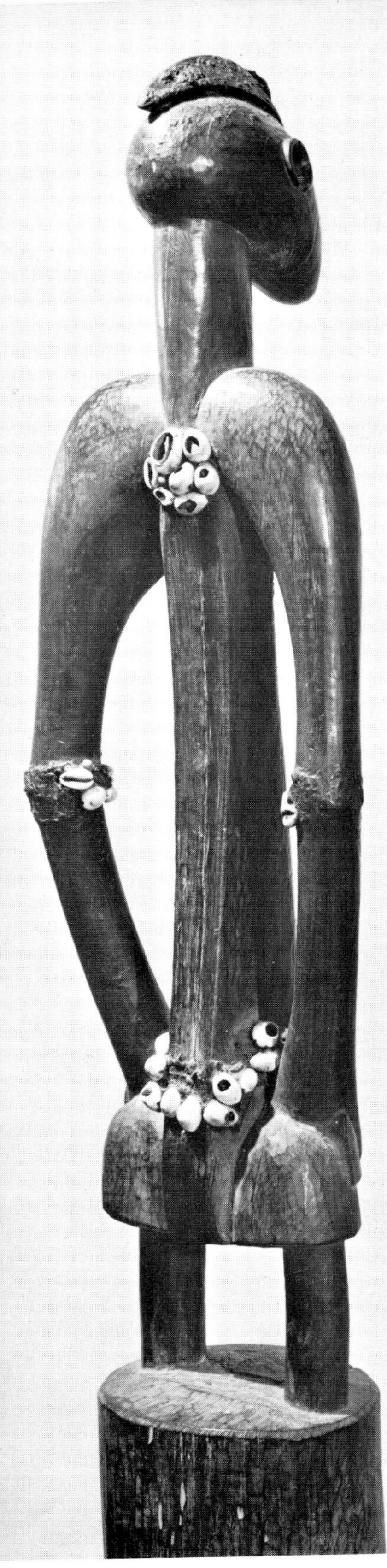

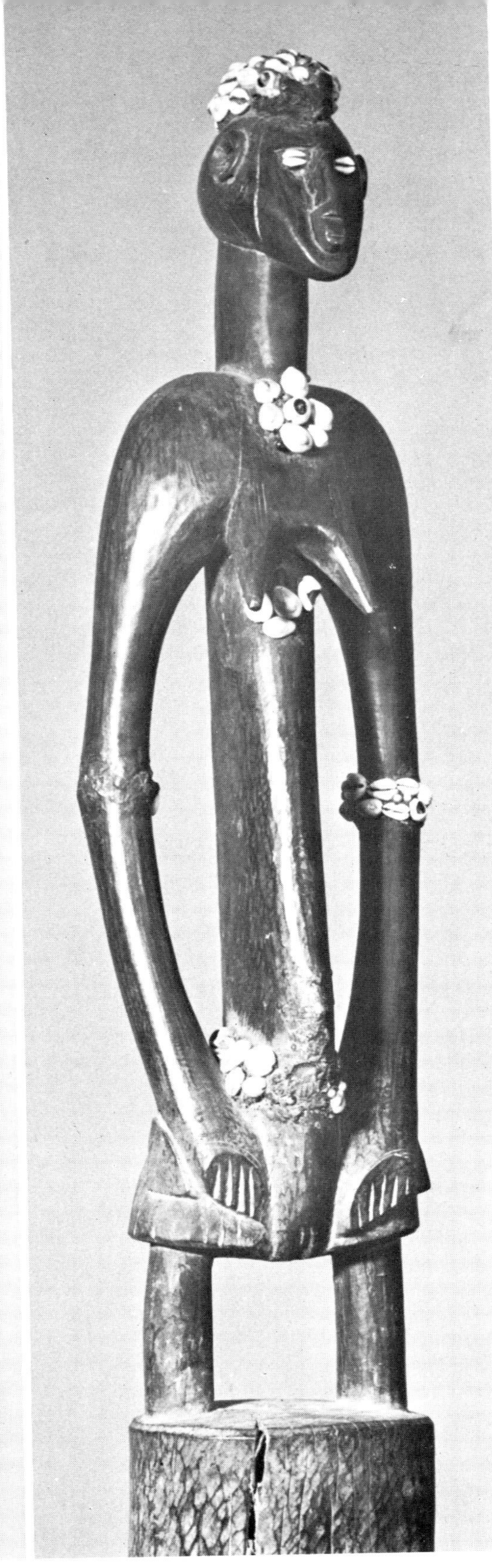

87a 87

88 88a

87, 87a Rhythm pounder, female (déblé). Northern region, Sikasso district [S: cf. no. 85]. Wood, cowries, 37½″ high. Collection Mr. and Mrs. Gustave Schindler, New York 88, 88a Rhythm pounder, female (déblé). Northern region, Sikasso district [S: cf. no. 86]. Wood, 36″ high. Collection Dr. Warner Muensterberger, New York 89 Rhythm pounder, male (déblé). Northern region, Sikasso district [A]. Wood, 35½″ high. Collection Mr. Pierre Verité, Paris 90 Rhythm pounder, female (déblé). Northern region, Sikasso district [S: cf. no. 89]. Wood, cowries, 31½″ high. Collection Mr. and Mrs. Allen Wardwell, Chicago

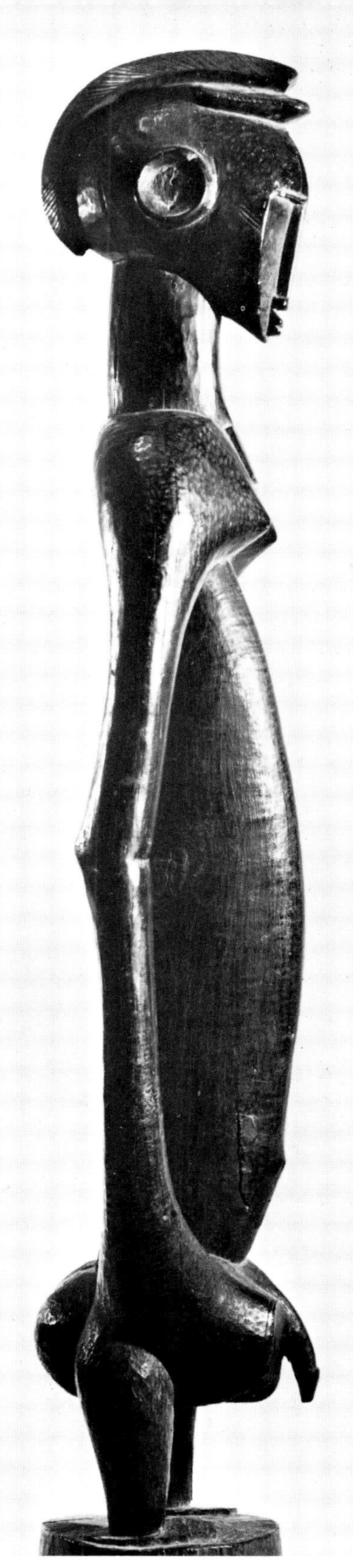

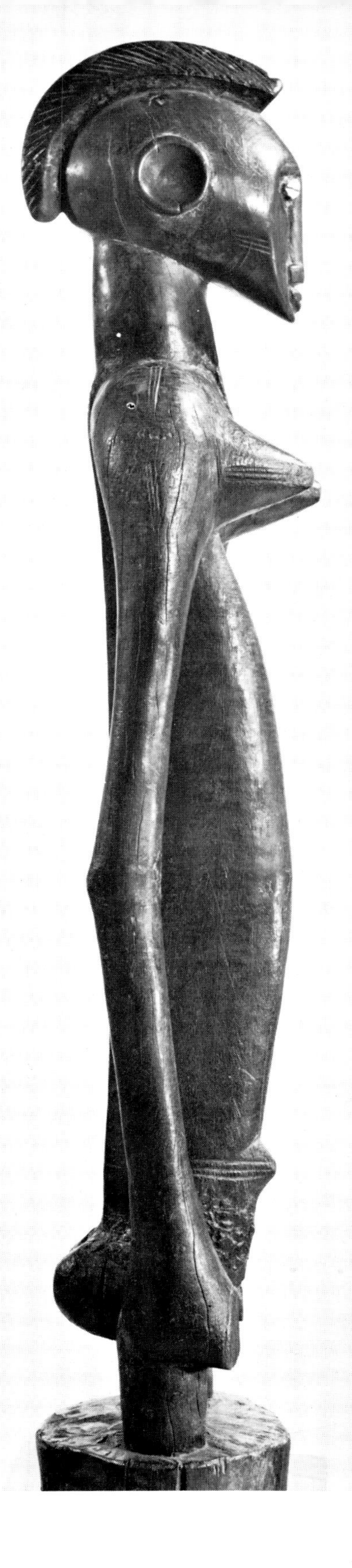

89 90

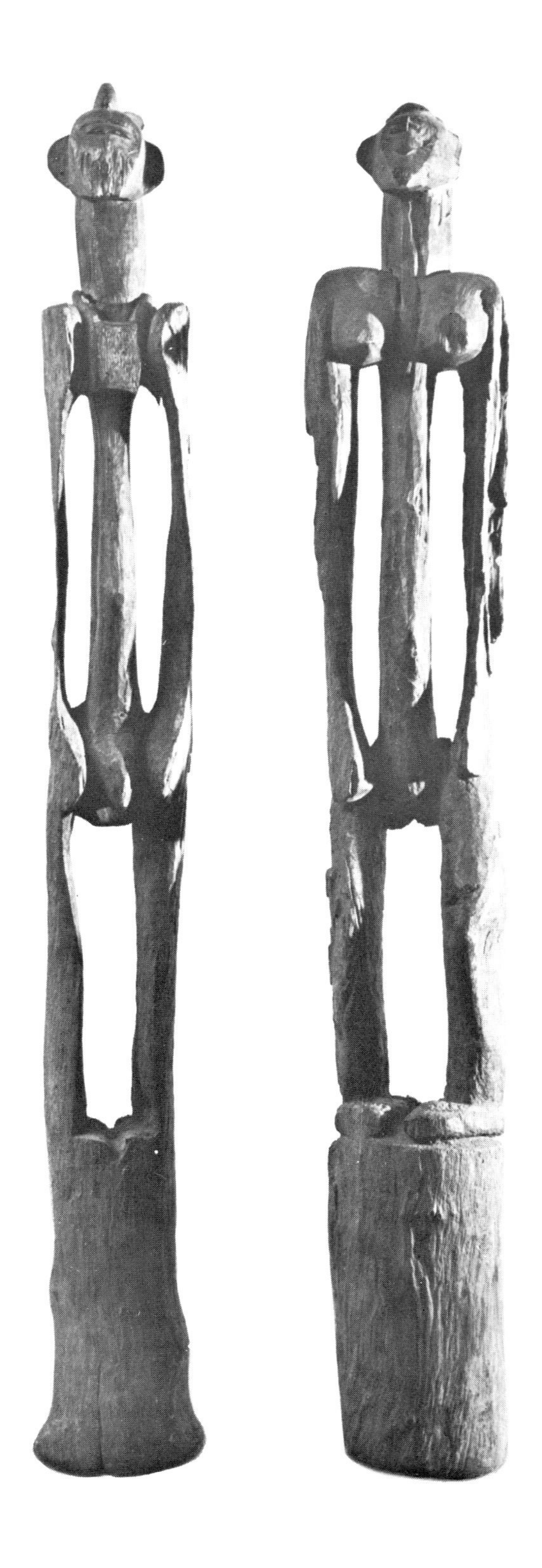

91

91a

91, 91a Pair of rhythm pounders (déblé). Northern region, San district? [A]. Male, wood, 46½" high; female, wood, 46" high. Collection Mr. R. Durand, Pau, France 92, 92a Rhythm pounder, female (déblé). Northern region, San district? [S: cf. no. 91]. Wood, 51¼" high. Collection Mr. Charles Ratton, Paris

92 92a

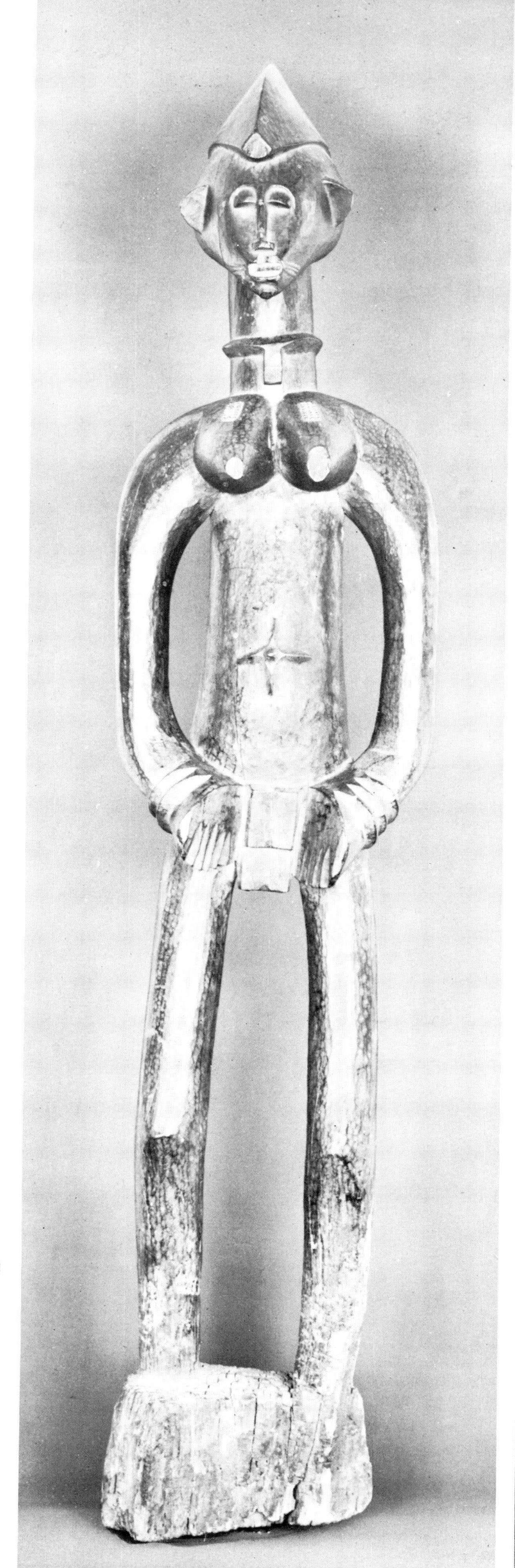

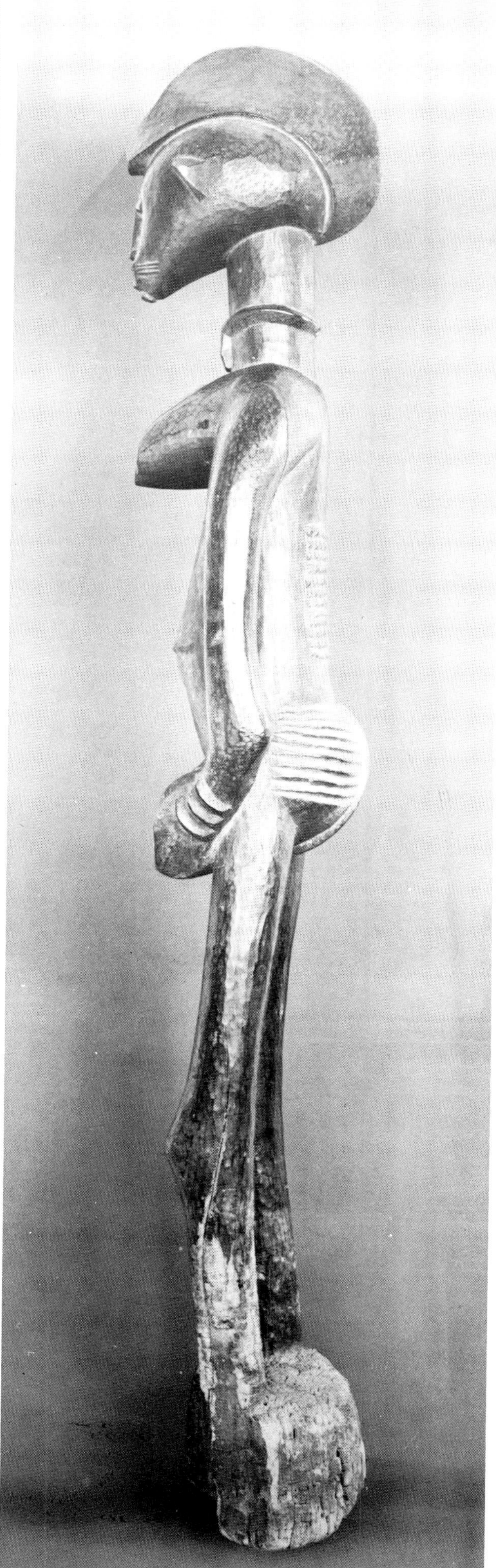

93 93a

93, 93a Pair of rhythm pounders (déblé). Northern region, San district? [S: cf. no. 91]. Male, wood, traces of paint, 45⅝" high. MPA 61.24; female, wood, traces of paint, 38⅛" high. MPA 61.25 94 Rhythm pounder, female (déblé). Central region, Korhogo district, Lataha village, Kiembara fraction [F: collected by Mr. Emil Storrer]. Wood, 37½" high. Museum Rietberg, Zürich RAF 301 95 Rhythm pounder, male (déblé). Central region, Korhogo district, Lataha village, Kiembara fraction [F: collected by Mr. Emil Storrer]. Wood, 42½" high. MPA 58.7

94 95

96 97

96 Standing female figure. Central region, Sinématiali village? [A]. Wood, 20¼" high. Collection Mr. Eric A. Peters, New York 97 Seated female figure with child. Central region [S]. Wood, 19½" high. Collection Mr. and Mrs. Gösta Wiberg, Stockholm 98 Equestrian figure. Central region [S]. Wood, 9¼" high. Collection Mr. Eliot Elisofon, New York 99, 99a Seated couple. Central region, Korhogo district [F: collected by Mr. F.-H. Lem near Sikasso, as coming from Korhogo]. Wood, 13" high. Collection Madame Helena Rubinstein, Paris

98

99 99a

100

101

102

103

104

100 Seated female figure. Central region [S]. Wood, 10¼″ high. Collection Mr. and Mrs. Milton Hirsch, Chicago 101 Seated female figure. Central region [S]. Wood, 21¼″ high. Collection Mr. Rudolf Indlekofer, Basel 102 Seated female figure. Central region [S]. Wood, 14″ high. Collection Mr. Chaim Gross, New York 103 Bowl, lid surmounted by seated female figure. Central region [A]. Wood, 7⅛″ high. Collection Dr. Hans Himmelheber, Heidelberg 104 Seated female figure. Central region [S]. Wood, 14″ high. Collection Mr. Ernst Anspach, New York

105 106

105 Seated female figure. Western region, Dembasso village, Niéné fraction [F: collected by Dr. Albert Maesen in 1939]. Wood, 10¾" high. Collection Professor Dr. P. J. Vandenhoute, Oostaker, Belgium IV 898 106 Standing female figure. Western region, Dembasso village, Niéné fraction? [S: cf. no. 105]. Wood, 6½" high. Buffalo Museum of Science C 13727 107 Seated female figure with child. Western region [A]. Wood, 35" high. Collection Mr. Paul Tishman, New York 108 Seated female figure with two children. Western region? [S]. Wood, 32¾" high. National Museum, Abidjan, Ivory Coast

107 108

109 109a

110 111

112

113 114

109, 109a Standing female figure. Central region [A: collected by Dr. Albert Maesen in 1939]. Wood, 6¾" high. Collection Dr. and Mrs. John Porter Foley, Jr., New York 110 Standing female figure. Central region? [S]. Wood, 10¼" high. MPA 56.224 111 Standing female figure. Central or western region [S]. Wood, paint, 19⅛" high. MPA 57.234 112 Standing female figure. Central region [S]. Wood, 8½" high. Collection Dr. Hans Himmelheber, Heidelberg 113, 114 Pair of standing figures. Central or western region [S]. Male, wood, 23½" high. MPA 60.163; female, wood, 23⅝" high. MPA 60.164

115 115a

116

117 117a

115, 115a Standing female figure. Northern region, Segou district [S: cf. Lem Pl.40. Bambara influence?]. Wood, 10¼" high. Ex collection Mr. Tristan Tzara, Paris 116 Seated female figure. Central region [S]. Wood, 8¾" high. Collection Mr. and Mrs. Harold Rome, New York 117, 117a Standing female figure. Northern region, Segou district? [S: cf. Lem Pl.40. Bambara influence?]. Wood, brass, 11⅜" high. Collection Mr. and Mrs. Irwin Hersey, New York

118 118a

118, 118a Standing female figure. Northern region? [S: Mossi influence?]. Wood, 6½″ high. Collection Mr. and Mrs. Raymond Wielgus, Chicago 119 Equestrian figure. Northern region [S: cf. no. 89]. Wood, 11″ high. Collection Mrs. Katherine W. Merkel, Gates Mills, Ohio 120 Standing female figure. Northern region [S]. Wood, cowries, beads, 6¾″ high. British Museum 1956 Af.27.39 121 Standing female figure. Northern region? [S]. Wood, 7½″ high. Musée de l'Homme, Paris 31.74.1726

119

120 121

122, 122a Standing female figure. Northern region [S]. Wood, 26⅛" high. Ex collection Mr. Louis Carré, Paris 123 Standing male figure. Northern region [S]. Wood, 35" high. Ex collection Mr. André Derain, Paris 124 Bowl, lid surmounted by standing female figure. Wood, 15¾" high. Brooklyn Museum, New York 61.91-1

122 122a

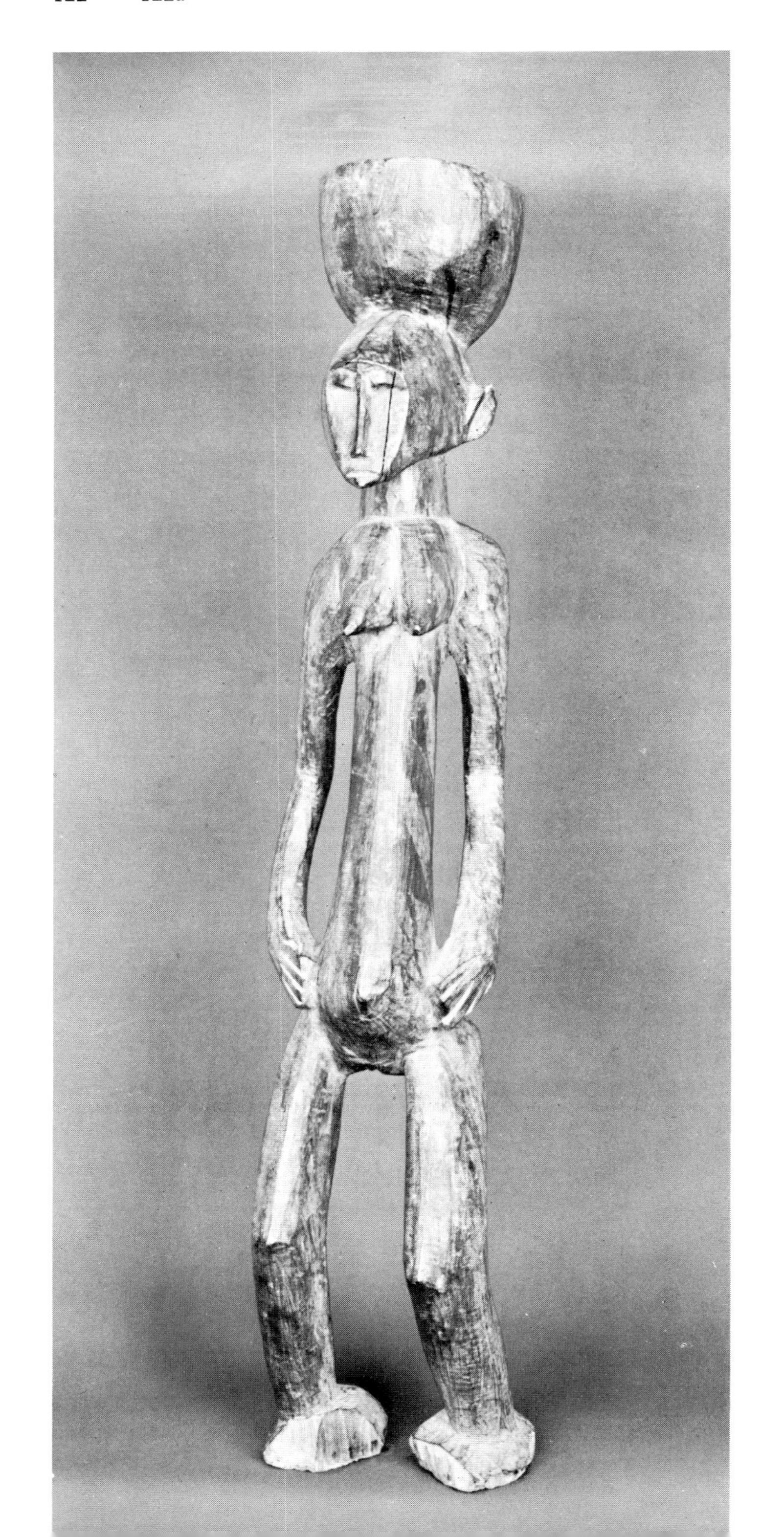

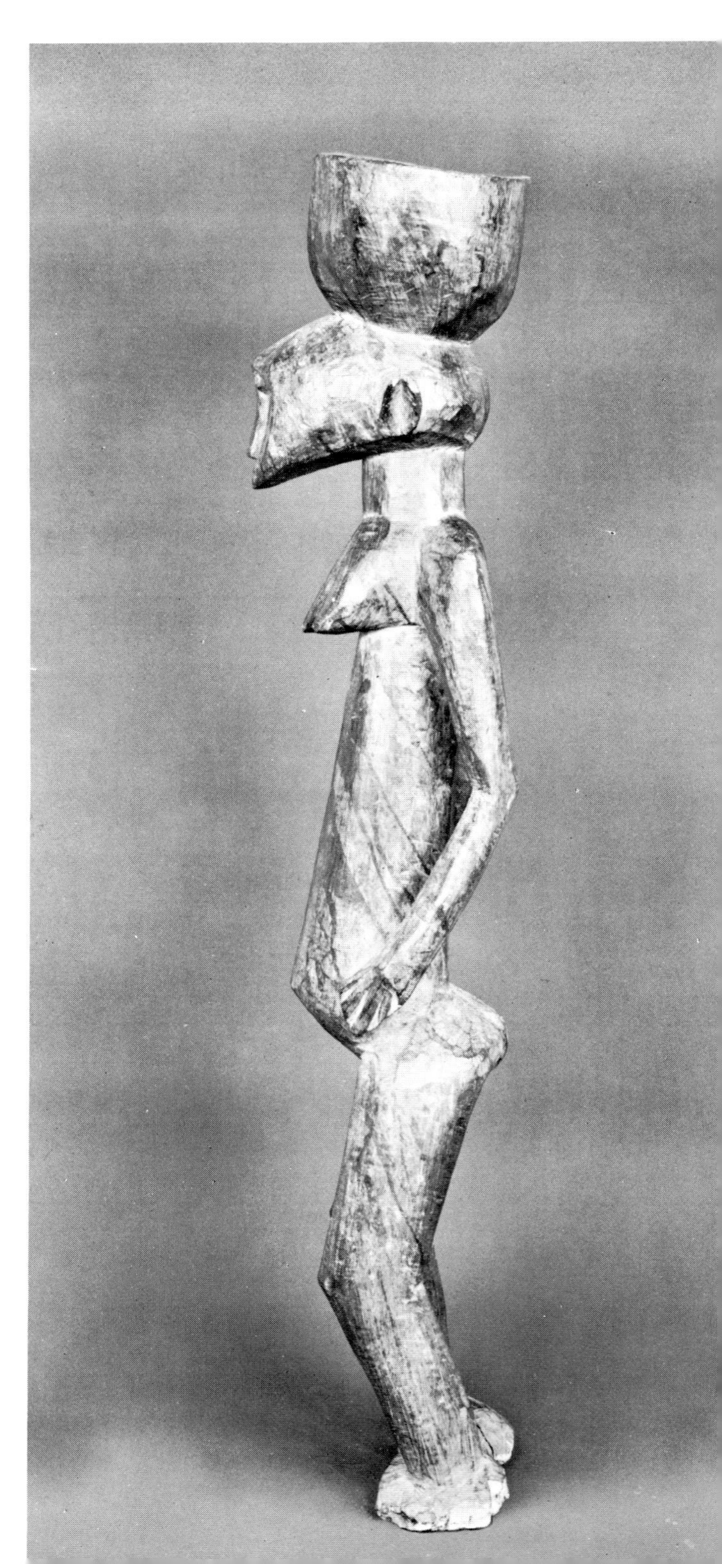

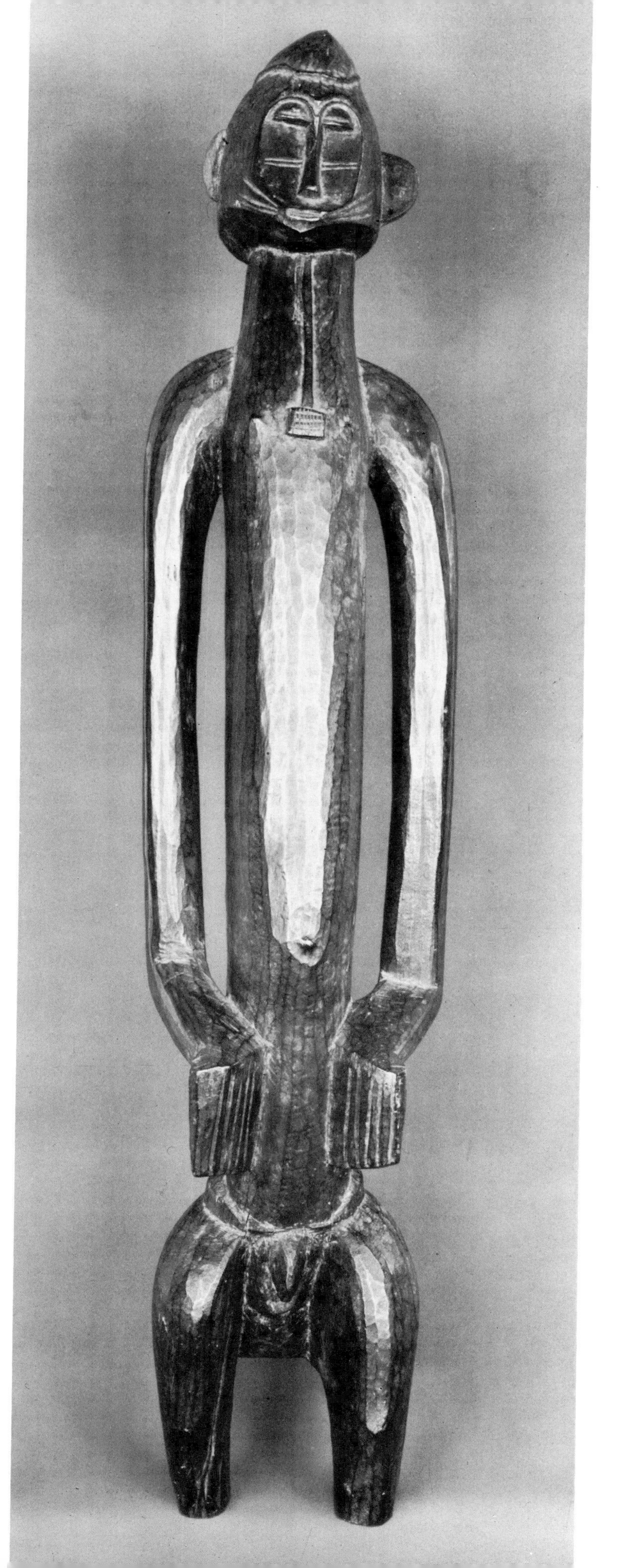

123 124

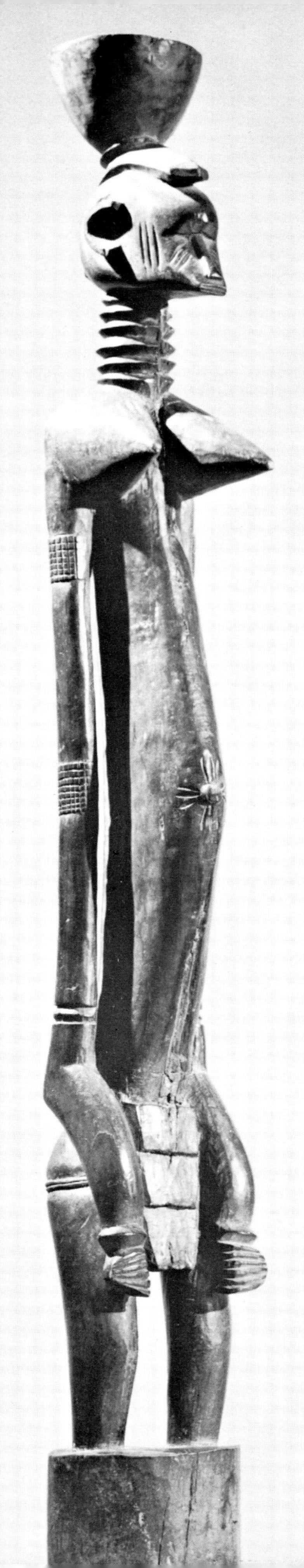

125 126

125 Rhythm pounder? (déblé?). Wood, traces of paint, 61¼″ high. Collection Mr. and Mrs. Henri A. Kamer, New York 126 Rhythm pounder? female (déblé?). Northern region, Sikasso district [S]. Wood, 34¾″ high. MPA 60.171 127 Standing female figure. Northern region [S]. Wood, 31¼″ high. Collection Mr. and Mrs. Arnold Newman, New York

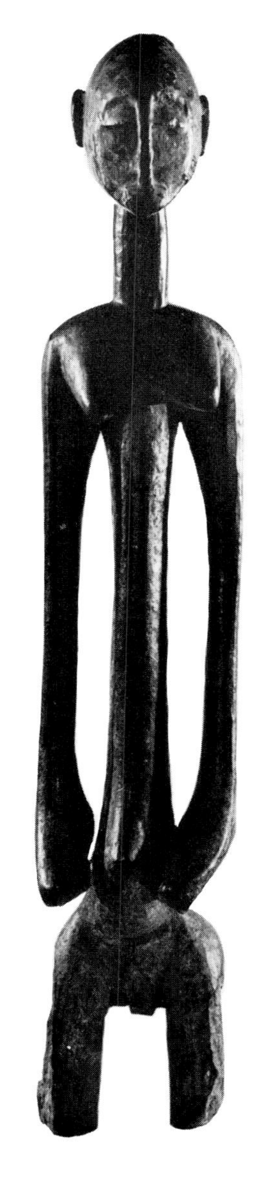

127

128 128a

129 130

128, 128a Staff with seated female figure (daleu). Central region [S]. Wood, iron, figure 10″ high, total height 55″. Collection Mr. Eric A. Peters, New York 129 Staff with seated female figure (daleu). Dyawala village, carver: Zambe [F: collected by Dr. Albert Maesen in 1939]. Wood, iron, traces of red paint, figure 13¾″ high, total height 60⅚″. Ethnographic Collections, University of Ghent IV 550 130 Detail of staff with seated female figure (daleu). Central region, Korhogo district? [S]. Bronze, figure 6⅞″ high, total height 41⅛″. Collection Mr. Charles Ratton, Paris

131 132 133

131 Detail of staff with seated female figure (daleu). Central region, Korhogo district? [S]. Bronze, iron, figure 5⅜" high, total height 48⅝". Collection Mr. and Mrs. Henri A. Kamer, New York 132 Detail of staff with seated female figure (daleu). Western region, Tyonyonkaha canton, Dyentene village, Kiembara fraction [F: collected by Dr. Albert Maesen in 1939]. Wood, 41⅜" high. Etnografisch Museum, Antwerp AE.55.37.16 133 Detail of staff with seated female figure (daleu). Western region [S]. Wood, figure 9⅞" high, total height 34½". American Museum of Natural History, New York 90.2-2753 134, 134a Detail of staff with seated female figure (daleu?). Northern region, Sikasso district [S]. Wood, figure 11" high, total height 35½". Collection Mr. and Mrs. Jean Verheyleweghen, Brussels

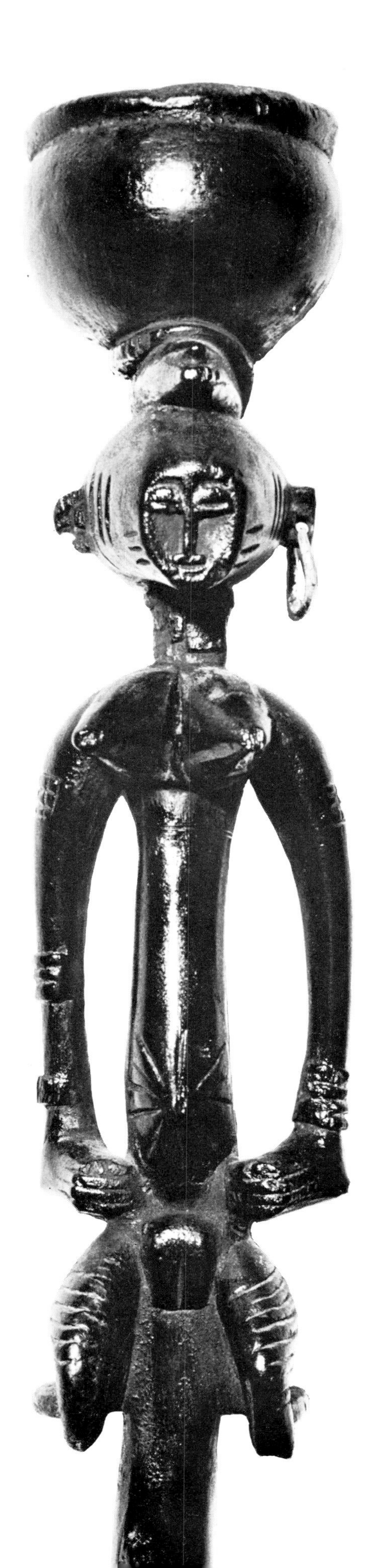

134 134a

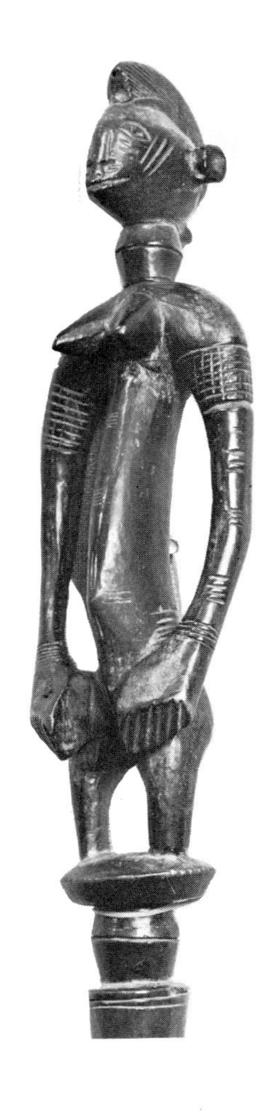

135 136

135 Detail of staff with standing female figure. Northern region, Sikasso district, belonged to King Babemba of Sikasso [A: collected in 1898]. Wood, figure 11½" high, total height 44½". Collection Galerie Le Corneur-Roudillon, Paris 136 Detail of staff with seated female figure (daleu). Wood, white paint, figure 16" high, total height 36½". Collection Mrs. Gertrud A. Mellon, New York 137 Group of flying birds. Wood, iron, brass, 19½" wide. Collection Mr. Aaron Furman, New York 138 Group of flying birds. Wood, iron, brass, 18¼" wide. Collection Mr. Joseph Floch, New York

37 138

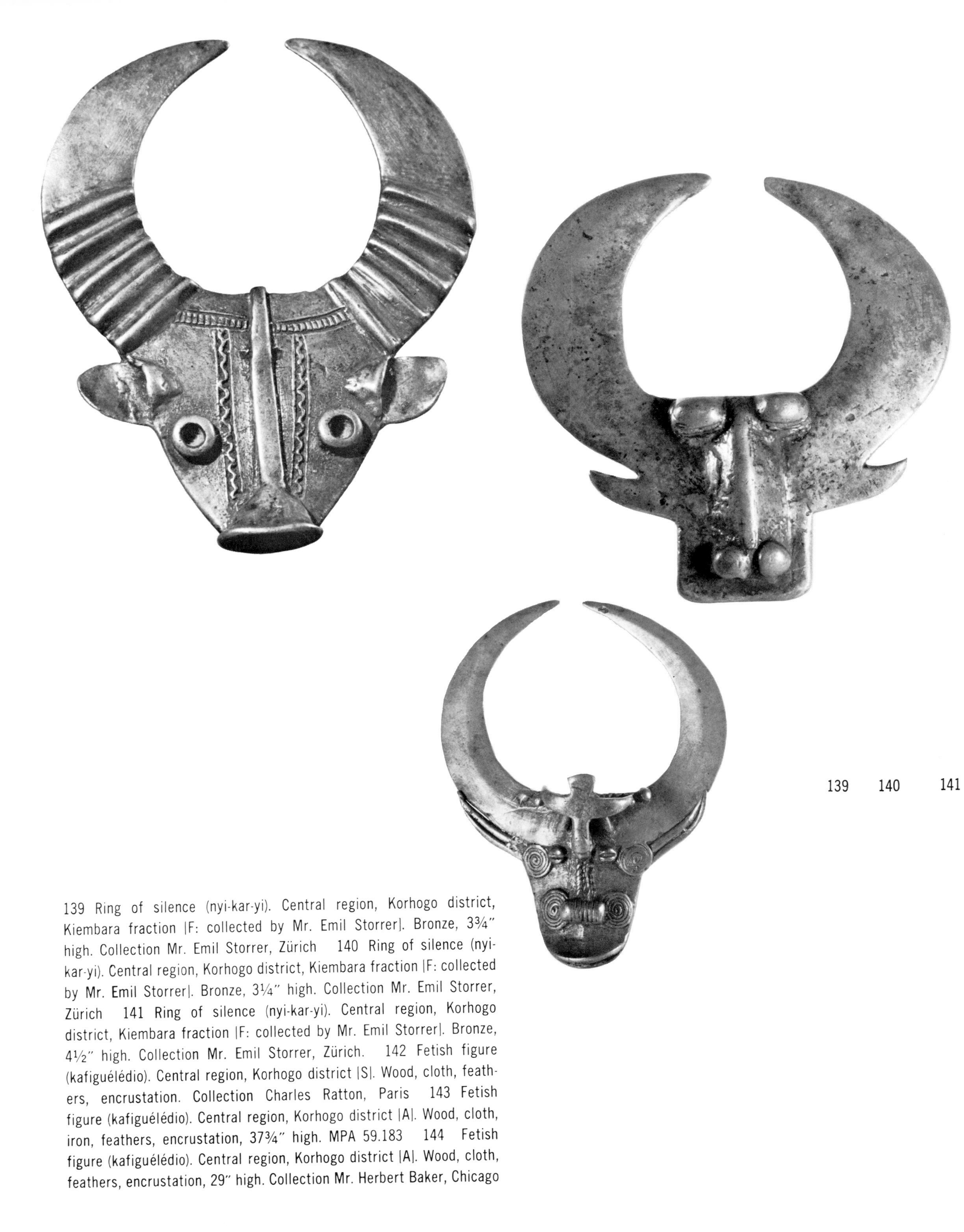

139 140 141

139 Ring of silence (nyi-kar-yi). Central region, Korhogo district, Kiembara fraction |F: collected by Mr. Emil Storrer|. Bronze, 3¾" high. Collection Mr. Emil Storrer, Zürich 140 Ring of silence (nyi-kar-yi). Central region, Korhogo district, Kiembara fraction |F: collected by Mr. Emil Storrer|. Bronze, 3¼" high. Collection Mr. Emil Storrer, Zürich 141 Ring of silence (nyi-kar-yi). Central region, Korhogo district, Kiembara fraction |F: collected by Mr. Emil Storrer|. Bronze, 4½" high. Collection Mr. Emil Storrer, Zürich. 142 Fetish figure (kafiguélédio). Central region, Korhogo district |S|. Wood, cloth, feathers, encrustation. Collection Charles Ratton, Paris 143 Fetish figure (kafiguélédio). Central region, Korhogo district |A|. Wood, cloth, iron, feathers, encrustation, 37¾" high. MPA 59.183 144 Fetish figure (kafiguélédio). Central region, Korhogo district |A|. Wood, cloth, feathers, encrustation, 29" high. Collection Mr. Herbert Baker, Chicago

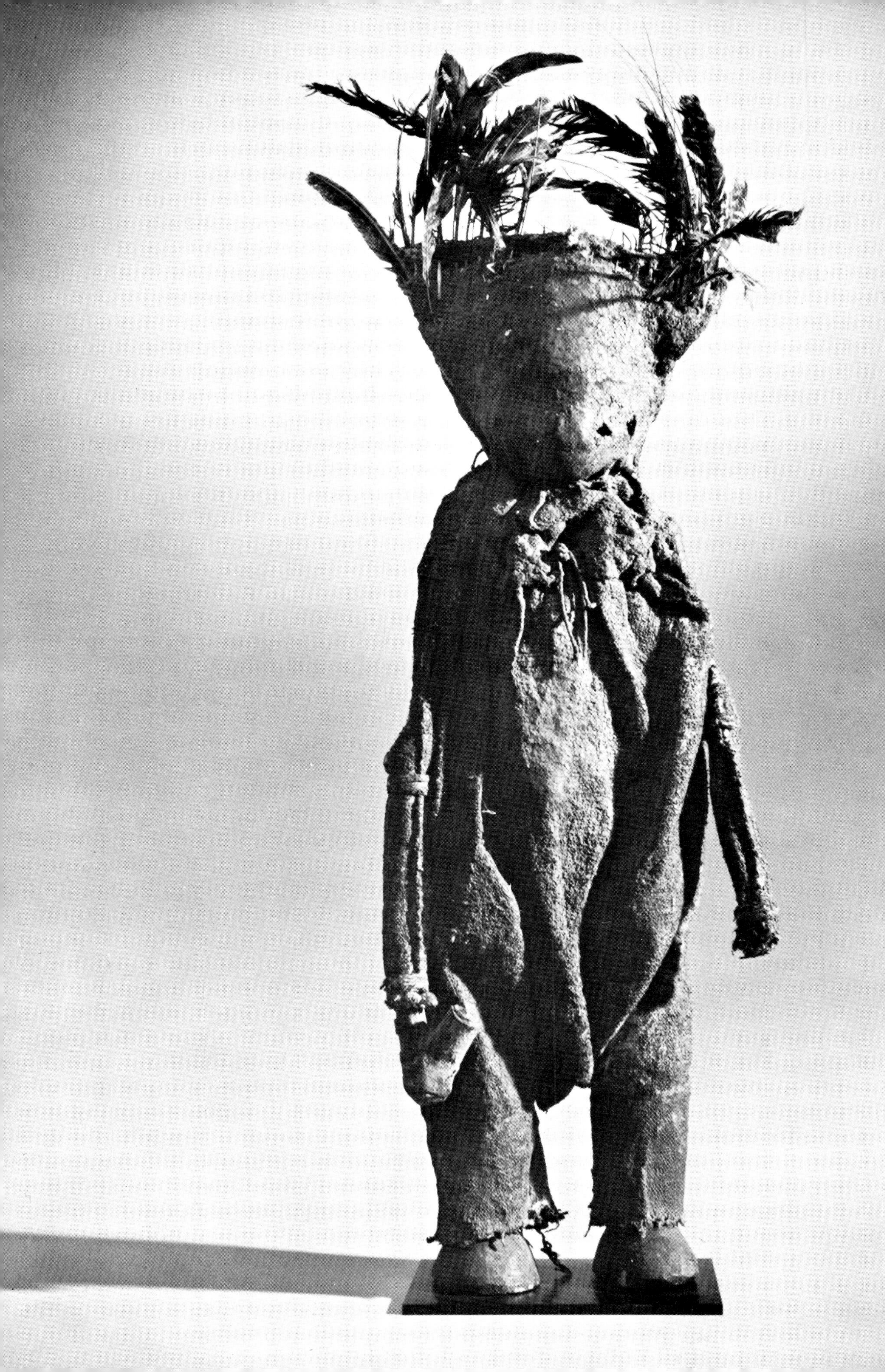

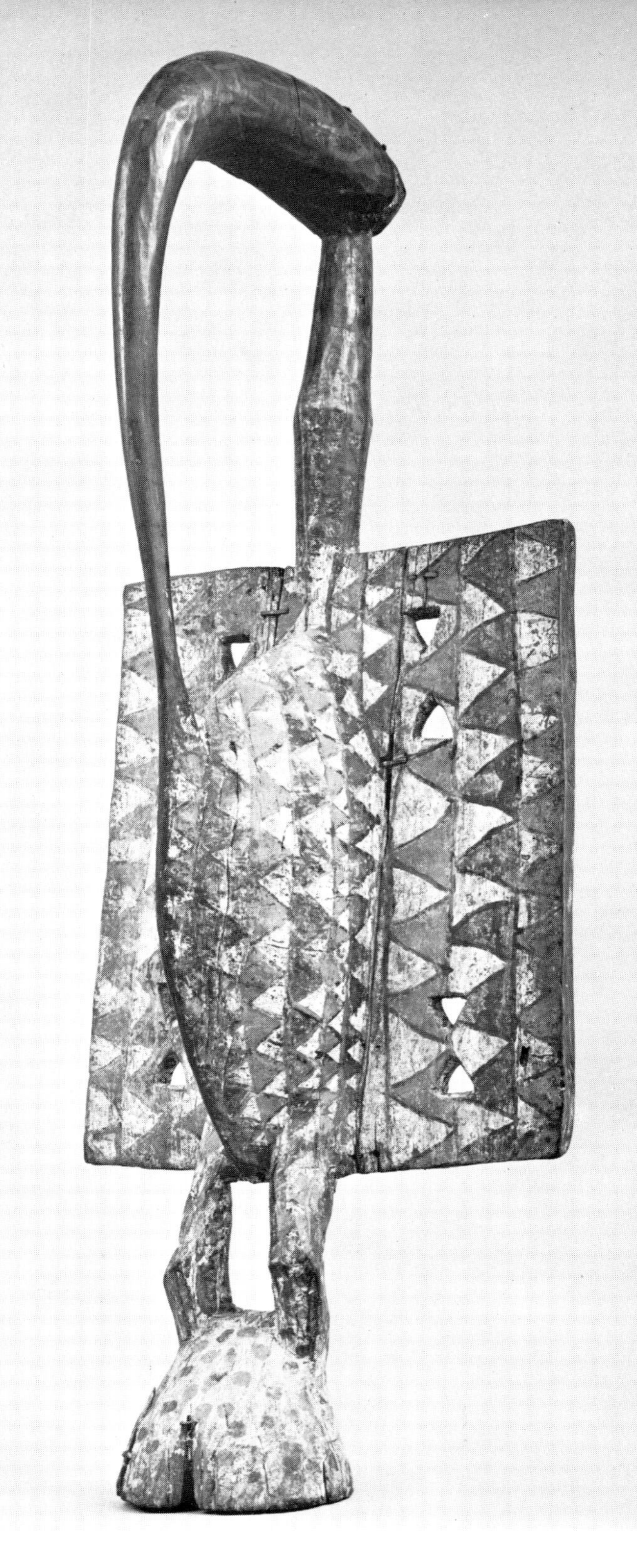

145 146 147

145 Bird (porpianong). Central region? [S]. Wood, paint, 57″ high. Collection Mr. and Mrs. Arthur A. Cohen, New York 146 Bird (porpianong). Central region? Wood, paint, 59⅝″ high. MPA 60.57 147 Bird (porpianong). Central region? [S]. Wood, 47½″ high. MPA 60.60

148 148a

148, 148a Bird (porpianong). Central region? [S]. Wood, 54″ high. Collection Mr. and Mrs. Henri Kamer, New York 149 Bird (porpianong) surmounting seated female figure. Central region? [S]. Wood, 63″ high. Collection Mr. John J. Klejman, New York

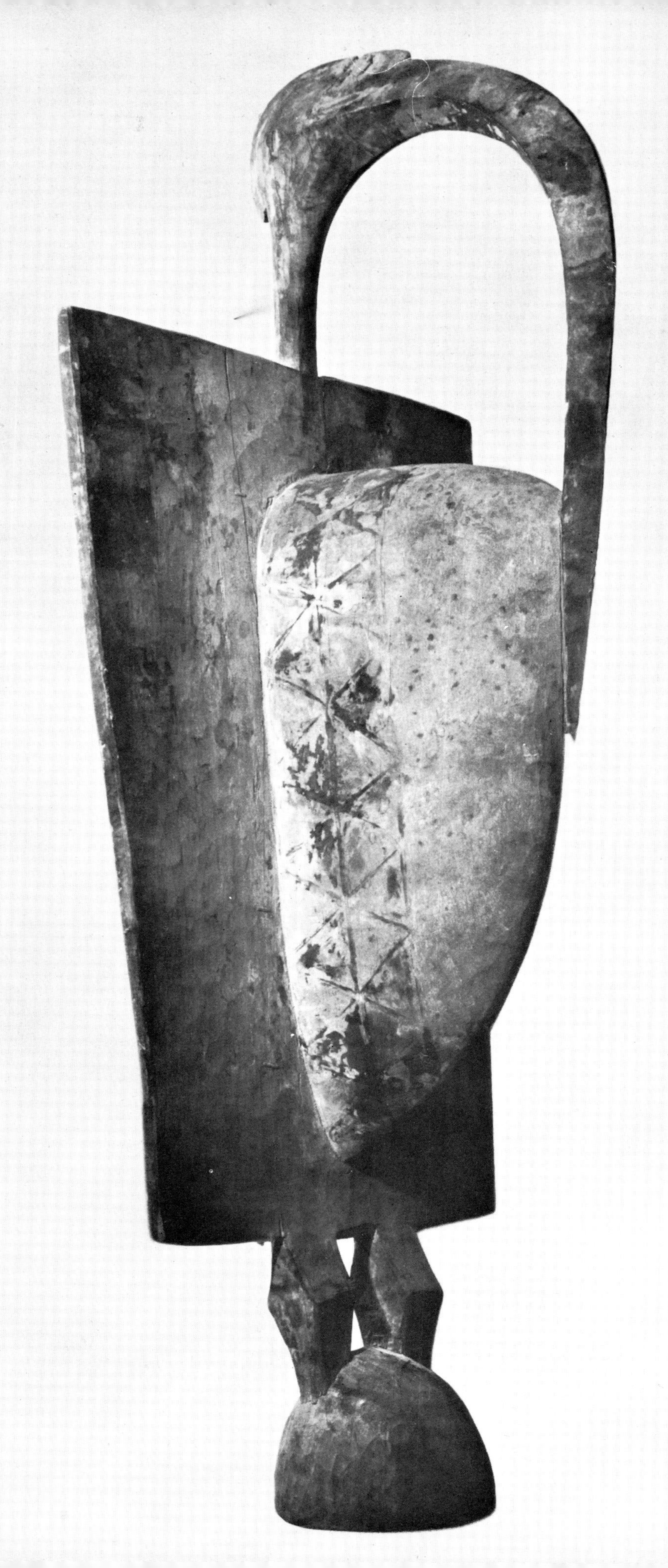

150

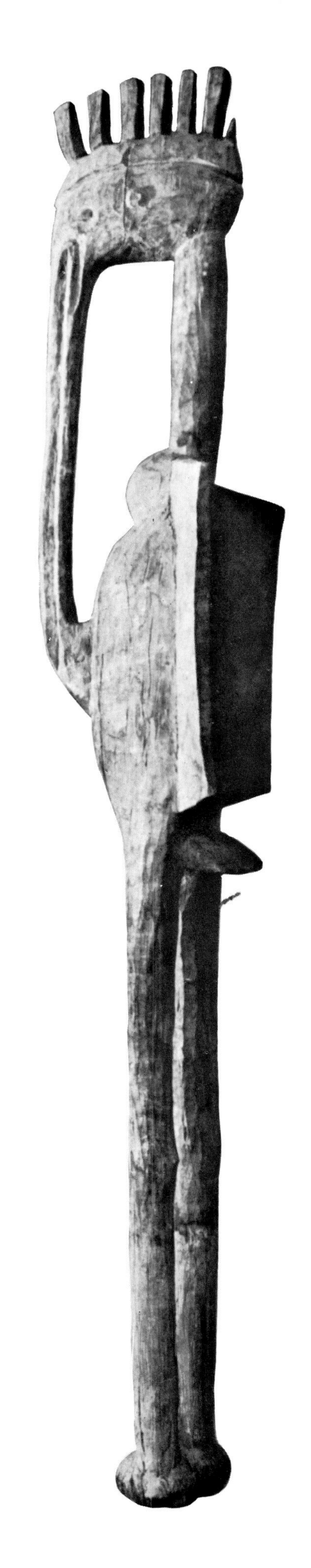

151

150 Bird (porpianong). Central region? [S]. Wood, traces of paint, 71¼" high. Collection Mr. Paul Tishman, New York 151 Bird (porpianong). Central region? [S]. Wood, 88¾" high. Collection Mr. Emil Storrer, on loan to Museum Rietberg, Zürich

152 153 154

155 156

152 Heddle pulley. Wood, 6⅛" high. Collection Mr. and Mrs. Harold Rome, New York 153 Heddle pulley. Wood, 6¼" high. Collection Mr. and Mrs. Harold Rome, New York 154 Heddle pulley. Wood, 6" high. Ex collection Dr. Stephen Chauvet, Paris 155 Heddle pulley. Wood, 6½" high. Collection Mr. and Mrs. Harold Rome, New York 156 Heddle pulley. Wood, brass, 7⅛" high. Collection Mr. and Mrs. Harold Rome, New York

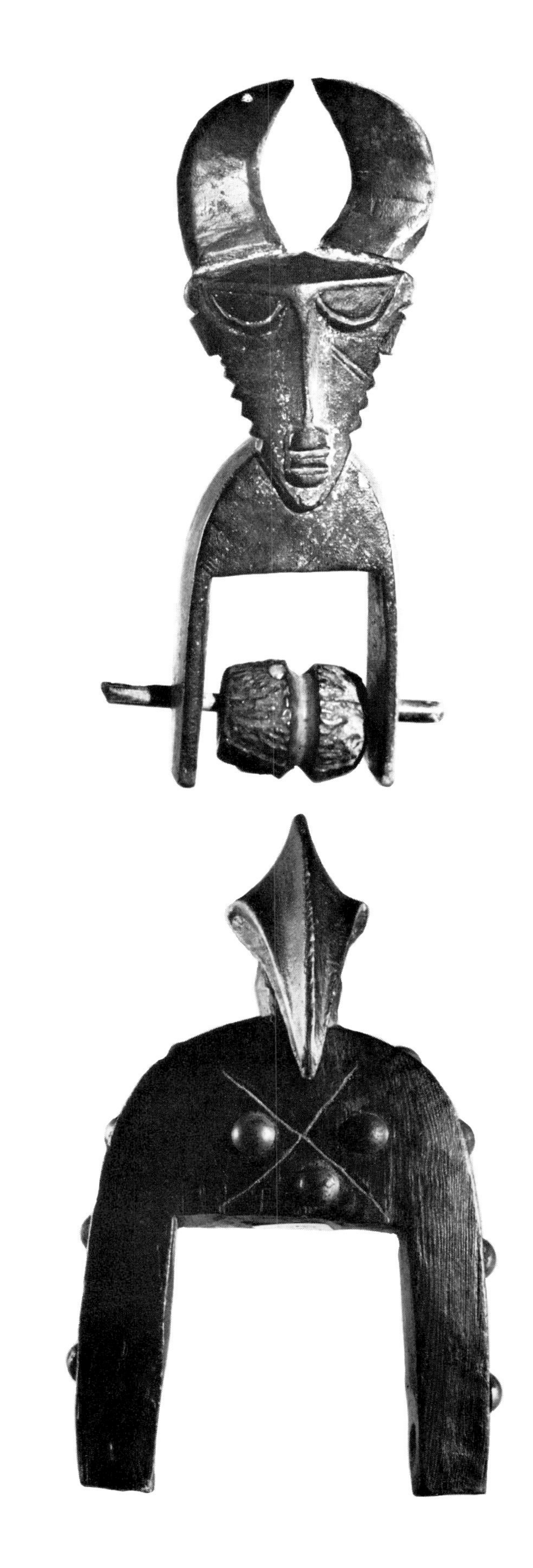

157

157 Door. Western region, Boundiali village [F: collected by Dr. Albert Maesen in 1939. Made in 1925 by carver Yalokone]. Wood, 61½″ high. Collection Mrs. Frans M. Olbrechts, Wezembeek, Belgium 158 Door. Central or western region [S]. Wood, 66½″ high. Collection Mr. and Mrs. Jean Verheyleweghen, Brussels

159

159 Door. Central or western region [S]. Wood, 54½″ high. Collection Mrs. Eugene Meyer, Mount Kisco 160 Door. Northern region? [S]. Wood, 45″ high. Collection Mrs. Alan H. Rosenthal, New York

161

161 Door. Northern region? [S]. Wood, 48″ high. Collection Mr. Ernst Anspach, New York 162 Door. Central region, Korhogo district [A]. Wood, 55¾″ high. Musée de l'Homme, Paris 62.23.2

162

163 164

163 Drum (pliéwo). Western region, Kouto district, Touvéré village, Niéné fraction [F: collected by Dr. Albert Maesen in 1939. Made in 1904]. Wood, hide, 34½″ high. Etnografisch Museum, Antwerp AE.55.30.25 164 Drum (pliéwo). Central region [F: photographed in situ by Dr. Hans Himmelheber]. Wood, hide, ca. 35½″ high 165 Drum (pliéwo) surmounting seated female figure. Central region [S]. Wood, hide, 48⅜″ high. Collection Mr. Charles Ratton, Paris

166 167

166 Part of a string instrument representing a female head. Western region, Boundiali district, Tiasso village, carver: Fonon [F: collected by Dr. Albert Maesen in 1938]. Wood, 7½″ long. Ethnographic Collections, University of Ghent IV 1266 167 Flute. Western region? Niéné fraction? [A]. Wood, 36″ long. MPA 62.129 168 Bird on top of a staff. Bronze, 5¼″ high, 5⅞″ wide. Collection Mr. Emil Storrer, Zürich 169 Detail of lamp (fitinne). Central region, Korhogo district, Sinématiali village, Naffara fraction [F: gift of chief Fandio to Father P. Knops in 1927. Said to be made in early 18th century]. Iron, bronze, 45″ high. Collection Father P. Knops, s.m.a., Brussels

68 169

170 171

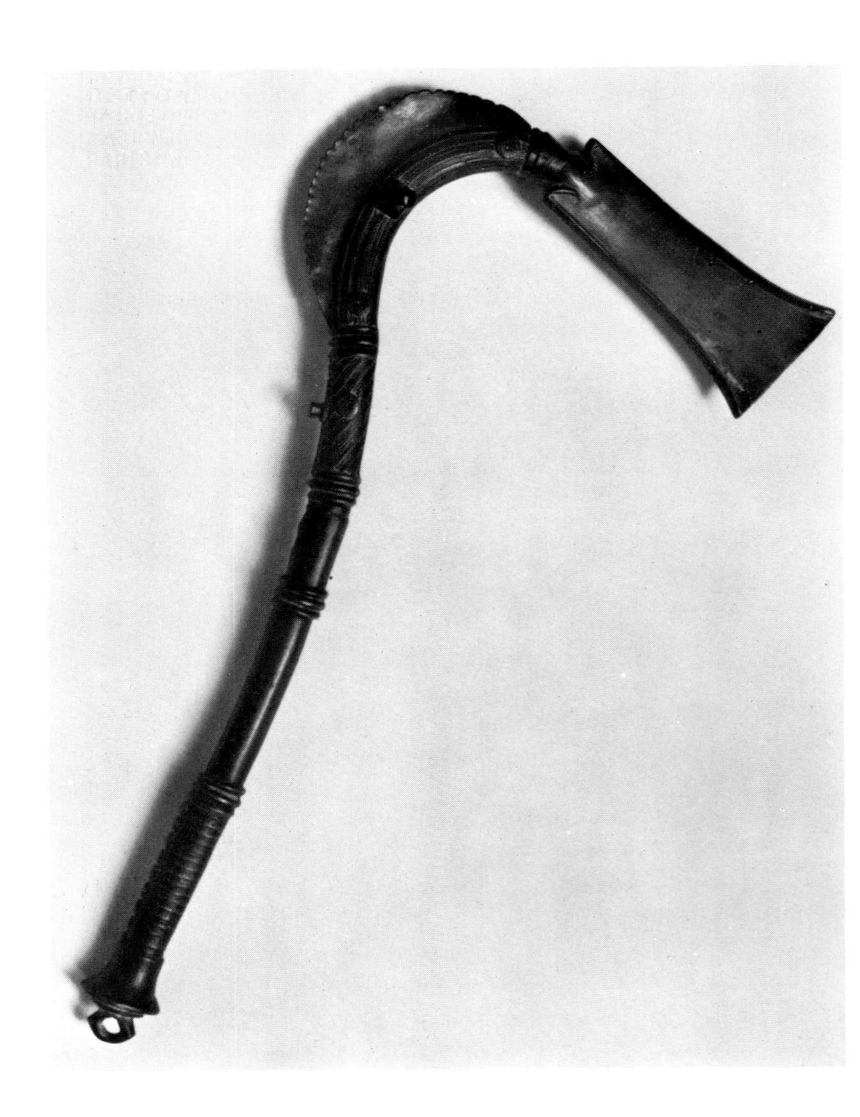

170 Game board. Central region [S]. Iron, 26" wide. Collection Carlebach Gallery, New York 171 Ceremonial axe. Central region, Ferkessédougou district, Soroko village, Nyarafolo fraction [A]. Bronze, 19¼" long. Collection Mr. Charles Ratton, Paris 172 Top part of a staff. Central region [S]. Bronze, 4½" high, 4¾" wide. Ex collection Mr. Tristan Tzara, Paris

172

173 Standing figure. Central region? [S]. Brass, 1⅝″ high. MPA 56.366 174 Standing figure. Central region? [S]. Brass, 2⅞″ high. Etnografisch Museum, Antwerp AE.59.55.60 175 Standing female figure. Central region, Korhogo district [A]. Bronze, 3⅛″ high. Collection Mr. and Mrs. Jean Verheyleweghen, Brussels 176 Standing couple. Central region? [S]. Male, bronze, 3⅛″ high; female, bronze, 3″ high. MPA 59.298a,b 177 Standing couple. Central region, Korhogo district [A]. Bronze, 2″ and 2⅛″ high. Collection Mr. and Mrs. Jean Verheyleweghen, Brussels

173 174 175

176

177

178 Carvers' section, Korhogo. Photo: Marc and Evelyne Bernheim, 1962

179 Market place, Abidjan. Photo: Marc and Evelyne Bernheim, 1962

180 Carvers' section, Korhogo. Photo: Marc and Evelyne Bernheim, 1962

Appendix: Modern Works

Sculpture "in the Senufo style" continues to be carved today. There are still some areas where this is genuine Senufo sculpture, executed in largely traditional ways for continuing traditional religious and social purposes. But this does not apply to most contemporary work which is made, in villages or in market places, for reasons of trade. The illustrations show something of the methods and results of this commerce. Masks and figures are manufactured on an assembly line basis, with carving, patination and artificial aging separated into distinct stages applied uniformly to a whole group of objects. Various styles (not Senufo alone), are imitated with indifferent success by artisans without any valid tribal background, and without knowledge of the cultural traditions which in the past infused the works with social meaning and esthetic coherence. Objects are made larger, and are elaborated by a combination of iconographic motifs now treated as purely decorative; the addition of such features as carefully-worked bases and sentimental gestures indicates the consciousness of their foreign destination.

Of these objects it must be said that not only are they no longer traditional Senufo sculpture, in a double sense they are not Senufo sculpture at all. Not issuing from ancient religious beliefs and social practices, not produced within their customary context, they are not intended to perform their traditional functions. This is a new kind of sculpture. One can then conclude on theoretical grounds alone that this sculpture must necessarily look radically different from the sculpture of the past, even if its artisans are related to their ancestors.

In affirming this it is not necessary to assume that the traditional 178 style, achieved at some long previous date, has been static, frozen in time and without its own development. With further information we 179 could undoubtedly follow its changes, and with further study this may yet be possible. But these changes—whatever they were—were gradual, effected either by contact with comparable cultures (Baule, Bambara, Dogon, etc.), or by the penetration of certain individual elements of more distant and distinct ones, notably Islam. They could therefore be absorbed, and contribute to the variations of Senufo style without 180 upsetting its underlying consistency. The new outside pressures are more destructive of ancient ways.

The actual appearance of the new work bears out the theoretical conclusion: it is fundamentally altered. When the process of mass manufacture or sale is illustrated the differences appear obvious; when the objects are isolated, either in Africa or out of it, they can

182 Standing figures [A: carved by the same workshop, probably by the same carver]. Female, wood, 35″ high. 63.268.57; female, wood, 40¼″ high. 63.268.68; male, wood, 37″ high. 63.268.67. Museum of Art, Indiana University

183 Mother and child. Wood, 31″ high. Museum of Art, Indiana University S62.75

181 Carvers' section, Korhogo. Photo: Marc and Evelyne Bernheim, 1962

181 in most instances still be detected. Crude workmanship is revealing, but modern craftsmanship can also be skillful. There are also altered 182 proportions, self-conscious, non-African gestures, or the exaggeration or multiplication of traditional features: braids of hair that join 183 the shoulders and help support the head. Sometimes bracelets are shown incised into the upper arm instead of being raised from it, or are so misunderstood and enlarged that the arm takes on the appearance of a bedpost. The neck of a figure may be suppressed, or scari- 184 fication marks become an over-all decorative pattern, extended at random. Other modern characteristics result from a radically-changed rendering of the human body and the relationship of its parts: individual features—mouth, eyes, hands or feet—are more naturalistic in detail, so that within each one lips and teeth, eyeballs and lids, knuckles and even fingernails call attention to themselves, while at the same time each larger part seems added on, rather than integrated into the rhythmic structure of the whole. Most difficult to 185 describe, but perhaps most fundamental, deft workmanship often serves a vision influenced by a foreign naturalism. The resulting change, elusive but unmistakeable, shows that the carver has a new desire to render the structural weight relationships of the human body accompanied by a consciousness of a relaxed, decorative flow of silhouette. Both of these concerns are outside traditional style.

That the careful observation of stylistic incongruities is a guide to modern origins can on occasion be confirmed by collateral technical knowledge. The rounded metal face mask is one such fortunate in- 186 stance. It presents several striking peculiarities: the large designs applied to forehead, cheeks and mouth; the relative size of the extended half-circles on either side of the face; the decorative banding on the double-curved legs; the impression of caricature conveyed by the whole design. These are all non-traditional characteristics. When chance turned up another mask, identical with the first except for slight changes in the appliqué, and so clearly cast from the same mold, this unorthodox procedure confirmed the mask's recent manufacture. The origin of other metal masks of related style or of exceptional materials must remain conjectural.

In another category are the deliberate and often well-meaning efforts to preserve past styles by the careful and conscientious copying of fine traditional works. The experience of similar attempts with many other styles (both in and out of Africa), suggests that even where these replicas seem identical with their models today, in all too short a time their differences will be entirely apparent.

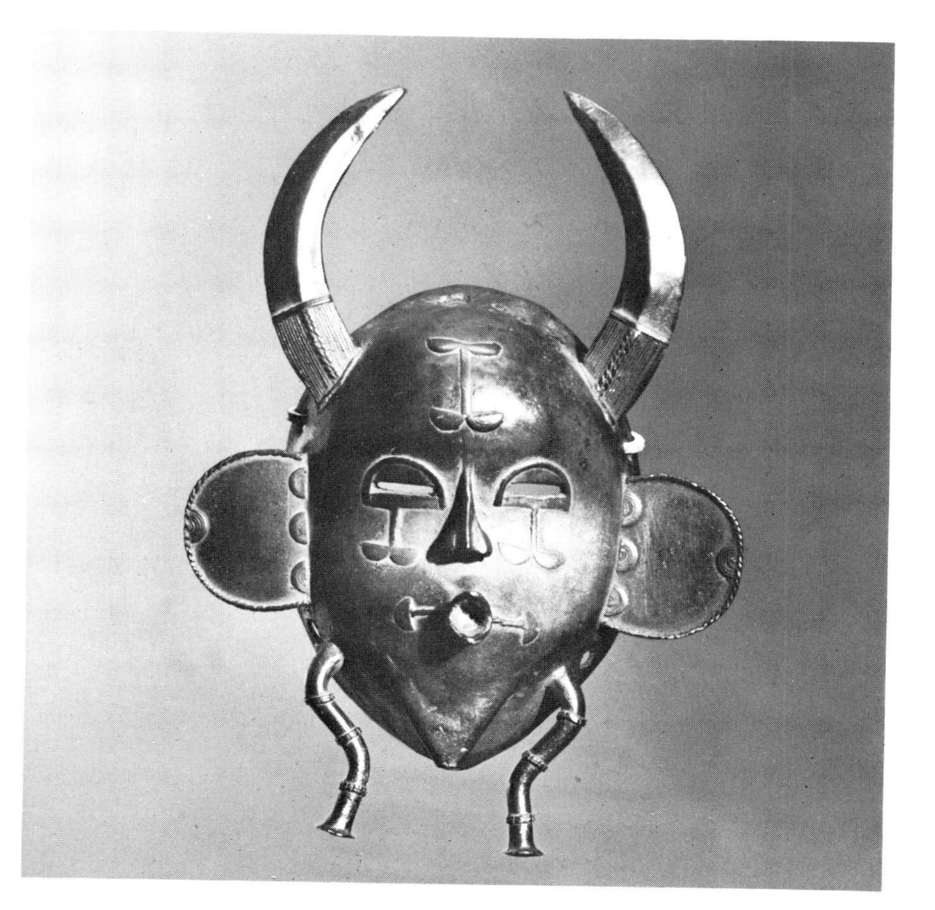

184 Mother and child. Wood, 34½″ high. Museum of Art, Indiana University S62.25

185 Standing female figure. Acquired in 1957. Wood, 33⅞″ high. Rijksmuseum voor Volkenkunde, Leiden 3432-1

186 "Face Mask." Copper, 11⅛″ high. Study collection, MPA 63.45. Gift of Henri and Hélène Kamer

Notes

1 Since most students of Senufo culture have written in French, their transcriptions of indigenous terms have been employed throughout—the spelling of "Senufo" excepted.
The summary of Senufo social structure is based on Holas, 1957a.
2 Holas, 1957a, p. 107.
3 Holas, 1957a, p. 145.
4 The description of the role of the lô society has been synthesized from Delafosse, 1908-1909; Vendeix, 1934; Clamens, 1953b; Holas, 1957a; Knops, 1956 and 1959.
5 Knops, 1959, p. 93.
6 Holas, 1957a, pp. 143-144.
7 Holas, 1957a, p. 150.
8 Vendeix, 1934, p. 639.
9 Knops, 1956, fig. 3, p. 160.
10 Clamens, 1953b, p. 78.
11 Delafosse, 1908-1909, p. 271; Vendeix, 1934, pp. 639-640.
12 Holas, 1957a, p. 152.
13 Holas, 1957a, p. 152.
14 Knops, 1959, p. 90.
15 Holas, 1960, p. 45.
16 Knops and Weyns, 1953, p. 68.
17 Lem, 1948, p. 18, suggests that he may be a "member of more ancient tribes, who once owned the soil."
18 Knops and Weyns, 1953, p. 69; Lem, 1942, p. 175; Himmelheber, 1960, pp. 94, 96.
19 Knops, 1959, p. 93.
20 Knops, 1959, p. 86; Knops, 1956, pp. 155-156.
21 Lem, 1948, p. 18.
22 Himmelheber, 1960, pp. 94 ff., who also says: "As among the Bambara, carving is done mainly by the smiths, so alongside the koulé the Senufo smiths also carve masks, large wooden vessels, and the handles of the iron tools they make." Holas, 1957a, pp. 40, 70, 169, 170; Holas, 1960, pp. 46, 51.
23 Lem, 1948, p. 18; Knops, 1959, p. 91; Himmelheber, 1960, p. 94; Holas, 1960, p. 45.
24 Knops, 1959, p. 101; Vandenhoute, 1948, passim; Gerbrands, 1957, passim.
25 Maesen, 1940, pp. 381-388.
26 Maesen, 1940, p. 230; Himmelheber, 1960, pp. 64-65, illustrates a comparable instance of extreme stylization of an originally naturalistic motif of the hair as occurring in a series of small figures of recent origin.
27 Maesen, 1940, pp. 232-233. Bochet's drawings as well as in situ photographs show the wearer's hands entirely free.
28 See below, in reference to the large ritual drums.
29 Holas, 1960, p. 60.
30 Holas, 1962, p. 20; Maesen, 1940, p. 382.
31 Maesen, 1940, pp. 383-387. He considers (p. 232) that the type with the human figure is of more recent origin, at least in the Korhogo (Kiembara fraction) area; elsewhere these distinctions do not apply.
32 Maesen, 1940, p. 387.
33 Holas, 1962, p. 20.
34 Holas, 1960, notes the existence of the double mask among the Koufolo fraction and suggests that it is confined to them.
35 Compare also another mask collected by Maesen with similar lip-plug and loop ornaments on the side, but surrounded by a kneeling female figure holding asymmetrical motifs one of which is the palm nut crest and the other a coiled crest. Illustrated Ghent, 1950, pl. 6.
36 Lem, 1948, p. 44, and pl. 50; he describes it as a "mask of totemistic character, representing the 'bird-woman' employed by the 'lô,' village confraternity, for its dances."
37 Freeman, 1898, p. 152 and ill.
38 Holas, 1960, p. 46. On the Bambara, see Goldwater, 1960, p. 17 and figs. 106-109.
39 Holas, 1960, p. 46. The exceptional materials of some metal masks (silver, copper and even aluminum), as well as certain decorative features associated with Islamic styles, also strongly suggest their recent origin.
40 The older view is exemplified in the comment of Delafosse, 1908-1909, p. 271, who, after referring to the "infantile state" of Senufo sculpture in general, continues: "C'est surtout dans la confection des masques religieuses que se révèle l'art indigène, et encore cet art, rustique dans l'exécution, conventionel dans l'invention, est-il tout à fait grossier."
41 Maesen, 1940, pp. 389-390.
42 Holas, 1962, pp. 15-16. In the Josef Müller collection, Solothurn, is a double mask very similar to that in The Museum of Primitive Art. See Bern, 1953, no. 93 and ill.
43 Holas, 1962, p. 14. Himmelheber, 1960, pp. 101, 103 assigns these masks to the lô society of the "farmer caste"; the single-muzzled ones from south of Korhogo, the double-muzzled from the west.
44 Prouteaux, 1918-1919, p. 38. Maesen, 1940, pp. 388 ff., suggests that besides chasing soul-eaters the masks may play a "political" role which, although less ostensible, may be their "real" function.
45 Prouteaux, 1918-1919, p. 48. He also points out, p. 51, that some of the older women, known as sorcerers, have on the contrary a certain connection with the demon mask, whose costume they prepare, and who must ask their permission to enter the village.
46 Prouteaux, 1918-1919, p. 48. Paulme, 1956, p. 43, follows Prouteaux, as does Leuzinger (1960, p. 95, and 1963, p. 76), but the mask illustrated is a kagba rather than the typical firespitter.
47 Prouteaux, 1918-1919, p. 48.
48 Maesen, 1940, p. 391.
49 Maesen, 1962. It must be noted that although Prouteaux and Maesen (at an interval of 25 years) are in entire agreement on the function of these masks, and the fact of "firespittting," their descriptions of its mechanism differ. Prouteaux evidently did not see sparks issue from the muzzle of the mask, while Maesen did. However, Maesen also says (1940, p. 238) that the masks were worn on the head like a helmet, with "the wearer seeing through the muzzle." If the muzzle was at eye height, how was it possible to blow sparks out through it?
In his 1962 communication Maesen confirms the substantial correctness of his information as published in the Philadelphia, 1956 catalogue, and adds: "All of the korubla masks and some of the other cult groups I managed to watch on the spot showed a coating of molten resin, if not of burned wood. In 1938-39 it was almost impossible to collect actually used specimens. None of the masks brought back showed traces of the molten resin used in 'firespitting.' " However, none of the many masks examined in 1963 at the time of the exhibition had any signs of charring, and only one, a mask probably too small to have been worn (Rubin collection) had anything other than a lightly painted surface, and its encrustation was not resinous.
50 Maesen, 1940, p. 389; Holas, 1960, pp. 56, 59, and fig. 17; Himmelheber, 1960, p. 103, and fig. 88b where it is called a lô mask of the "blacksmith

caste" from south of Korhogo—(there also being a horned variety west of Korhogo). Maesen also describes a similar mask representing a monkey, unknown in the central area but frequent in the west, which is used in a pantomime dance of purely recreative intention.

51 Maesen, 1940, p. 241; Lem, 1948, p. 44, and pl. 51.

52 Lem, 1948, p. 45, and pls. 54 and 55.

53 Elisofon and Fagg, 1958, fig. 109.

54 Knops, 1956, p. 159, who, however, does not distinguish between kagba and nassolo.

55 We owe this description to Mr. Bochet's own commentary, kindly communicated with his drawings.

56 Holas, 1957a, p. 152, who quotes Bochet; and Holas, 1960, pp. 59-60, where his description follows Bochet's drawings.

57 Bochet, quoted by Holas, 1957a, p. 150, and Bochet's commentary accompanying the drawing illustrated here.

58 Knops, 1956, p. 158.

59 These impressive works have only recently come to light. They are nowhere mentioned in the literature.

60 Clamens, 1953b, p. 78, and fig. 4.

61 Holas, 1957b, p. 35, and fig. 4; Holas, 1960, p. 56.

62 Holas, 1962, p. 13.

63 Lem, 1948, p. 44, and pl. 45. For a series of dramatic views see Elisofon and Fagg, 1958, fig. 96.

64 Lem, 1948, p. 43, and pl. 44.

65 Pau, 1961, no. 109, and pl. 14. The character of the wood, light-colored and hard, bears out this provenance.

66 In 1935 this work, then in the Carré collection, was no. 64 in the exhibition African Negro Art. See New York, The Museum of Modern Art, 1935.

67 Leuzinger, 1963, p. 64, fig. 23a, b, c. Although collected as a functional pair (male and female), and so presumably carved as such by the same sculptor, one may properly question whether these two figures were executed by a single hand. In their present state the bodies are difficult to compare, though the Rietberg figure seems more massive. But even allowing for changes produced by weathering, the rendering of the heads, their size and relation to the body are very different. The third pounder, is now in the Josef Müller collection, Solothurn (Bern, 1953, no. 86, and ill.). Storrer concludes that because the three come from Lataha village all "must be by the same carver."

68 Holas, 1957b, p. 30, and figs. 1-3.

69 Holas, 1957b, p. 30.

70 Holas, 1957b, pp. 30, 35.

71 Himmelheber, 1960, p. 108.

72 Maesen, 1940, pp. 363-365. He describes an "important" representation of a male figure with a snake winding over its shoulders and torso, made in the Korhogo region. No examples of this figure have come to light.

73 Lem, 1948, p. 44, and pl. 46.

74 Maesen, 1940, pp. 365-367; Clamens, 1953a, p. 14; Clamens, 1953b, p. 79.

75 Maesen, 1940, p. 361. These rings are to be distinguished from the rings of silence connected with initiation ceremonies. Clamens, 1953c, p. 107, explains the yirigefolo as one of the loho syene, or water spirits who are creators. The animals (yawige) represented in the metal ornaments—python, crocodile, tortoise, etc.—function as intermediaries for the creators and for this reason are not to be eaten; the figures remind the owner of the taboo.

76 Knops and Weyns, 1953, pp. 63-65, and the illustrations reproduced here with Father Knops' kind permission.

77 Lem, 1948, p. 44, and pl. 46.

78 Kjersmeier, 1935, pl. 32; Lem, 1948, p. 43, and pls. 40 and 41. The Tzara figure was no. 58 in New York, The Museum of Modern Art, 1935; London, British Museum, 1953, p. 22, and pl. 14.

79 Kjersmeier, 1935, pls. 38, 39. A seated figure carrying a jar (pl. 41) is also in this style.

80 Guillaume and Munro, 1926 , fig. 19. New York, The Museum of Modern Art, 1935, nos. 2 and 66. No. 2 (our illustration 123) was reproduced in Basler, 1929, pl. 33a. Kjersmeier, 1935, p. 29: "Pour les enterrements, deux grandes statuettes de sexes différents sont placées sur la place publique du village; sur la tête, elles portent une coupe dans laquelle des offrandes de cauris sont déposées." (Paulme, 1956, p. 42, follows Kjersmeier.) This description seems applicable to the figure now in the collection of The Museum of Primitive Art (fig. 126) as well as the former Carré figure, except that Kjersmeier adds that these tall figures (about 1 meter high) are generally "peu soignées." The figure formerly in the Derain collection may be a rhythm pounder with the base now missing.

81 Holas, 1962, p. 9. On the basis of internal evidence, there would appear to be some question as to whether the metal staffs were ever intended for true ceremonial usage. Compared to the small divination figures, and such other old metal work as Father Knops' lamp, they are extremely finely cast with a technique available only in the larger centers, and that perhaps for not too long a time. However, Clamens, 1953a, does report such a metal staff.

82 Knops and Weyns, 1953, pp. 62-63, who call them "vrouwtje van de landman," report them as given to the 18 to 22-year old (i.e., the oldest) age group. Maesen, 1940, pp. 376-378, says that in the west the oldest group receives them, while in the central region it is the youngest group. He mentions that these trophy figures sometimes occur without the staff; Knops and Weyns illustrate such a seated figure, as does Kjersmeier, 1935, pl. 40, who calls it "femme assise en usage dans la société d'agriculture . . ." Himmelheber, 1960, p. 108, includes mother and child groups. On the Bambara, see Goldwater, 1960, pp. 15-16.

83 Clamens, 1953a, p. 14. "De cette croyance aux nains-génies, il faut rapprocher l'usage des bâtons de culture, nommé ndewu, ndebele, pygmée ou lutin. C'est une canne au sommet de laquelle trône un petit personnage. Lorsqu'on cultivent les champs, le bâton est placé à l'extremité du terrain de le premier qui a fini son sillon, saisit le bâton et se met à danser avec lui; hommages certains aux génies de la terre, aux pygmées, premiers occupants." Knops, 1958, p. 116, employs these same terms, but also (1959, p. 102) refers to "bâtons d'initiation pour les filles, ou daléu."

84 Holas, 1960, p. 51.

85 Maesen, 1940, pp. 350, 378-379, who says they are given as trophies to the older age groups; and Knops, 1958, p. 120. Elisofon and Fagg, 1958, p. 56, also mention that "cult houses of clans were sometimes surmounted by wooden birds."

86 Lem, 1948, pp. 26, 44, and pl. 49.

87 Our account follows the detailed description given by Storrer, 1962, in an unpublished article accompanied by photographs he took. Father Clamens' article (1953d) describes the Nyi-kar-yi (literally: those who change themselves into cows), as an association of healers, among the Kiembara in the Korhogo district, who are said to be able to turn themselves into cows which trample on the crops, and to be immune to firearms, and who can, in fact, heal sores, fractures, mad-dog and snake bite. The ring (which takes its name from the association), "is worn on the finger during certain ceremonies, but is held firmly clenched between the teeth during funeral

rites . . . thus imposing a silence which is required of members of the association. [The ring] is the property of the association; at the death of the holder it will go to a new member." Father Clamens publishes the three rings illustrated here, four others of the same bovine shape, and two that are closer to Storrer's photograph; all were given to Massa in the village of Watyene. Knops, 1958, p. 120, follows Clamens in his characterization of the nyi-kar-yi. Himmelheber, 1960, p. 99, and fig. 87, follows Storrer, but refers to "a week's silence," rather than "six days in the bush."

88 Holas, 1960, p. 51; and Holas, 1962, pp. 6-7: "The kafiguélédio has only a relatively limited horizontal extension, being found, so far as one knows, above all among the Kiembara, Koufolo, Kafimbélé, as well as among certain Naffara and Niarafolo."

89 Holas, 1960, p. 51. Maesen, 1940, p. 374, noted that in 1933 Frans Olbrechts had collected a "dangerous magic" standing male figure carrying a heavy stick. This may well have been an example of the kafiguélédio. It must also be remarked that Maesen records kafegeledyg as the name of a well-meaning spirit, opposed to the ndebele which are bad, while Father Clamens (1953a) gives ndebele, meaning pygmy, as one of the names of the agricultural staffs, or daleu.

90 Holas, 1960, p. 57. Leuzinger, 1963, p. 70, calls the calao "the founder of the Senufo society," and describes the typical sétien illustrated there as having "features of an ibis, a pelican, a hornbill, and a stork or cock."

91 Holas, 1960, p. 59, and 1962, p. 11.

92 Maesen, 1940, p. 402, reports contradictory information given for the bird, said to symbolize the ancestors and also to be a symbol for the male. Holas's analysis would seem to reconcile the two.

93 It is also possible that those birds on bases are of a later style, but there is at the present time no way of determining this.

94 Knops, 1956, p. 154: "Le tisserand est au contraire un homme de métier. Parce que le tissage est d'importation étrangère et récente, il n'est pas abrité derrière un rideau opaque de traditions, croyances et tabous comme l'est au contraire la fonction de forgeron. Bien que le forgeron soit de tradition, le tailleur de bois, le tisserand a le droit de fabriquer son métier, de décorer la navette, le blanc d'os, la poulie du métier."

95 Information kindly transmitted by Jacqueline Delange (1963), to accompany the door in the Musée de l'Homme (fig. 162); and Maesen, 1940, pp. 395-396, 403.

96 Information gathered in the field by Maesen, 1938-1939, as reported by Vandenhoute, 1962.

97 The University Museum door is fig. 5 in Elisofon and Fagg, 1958.

98 This door was No. 168a in the 1935 exhibition of African Negro Art at The Museum of Modern Art, but is not listed in the printed catalogue.

99 Clamens, 1953b, pp. 76-78; Maesen, 1940, p. 400.

References

Basler, Adolphe
1929 L'art chez les peuples primitifs. Paris.

Bern. Kunsthalle
1953 Kunst der Neger, 24. Oktober—26. November. [Ausstellungskatalog von Werner Schmalenbach] Bern.

Bochet, Gilbert
1962 Communication, October 17.

Clamens, Gabriel
1953a Curieuse statue de cuivre sénoufo. Notes africaines, 57:14.
1953b Notes d'ethnologie sénoufo. Notes africaines, 59:76-80.
1953c Dieux d'eau en pays sénoufo. Notes africaines, 60:106-108.
1953d Les Nyi-kar-yi de Watyene. Notes africaines, 60:108-110.

Delafosse, M.
1908-1909 Le peuple Siéna ou Sénoufo. Revue des études ethnographiques et sociologiques, 1:16-32, 79-92, 151-159, 242-275, 448-457, 483-486; 2:1-21.

Delange, Jacqueline
1963 Communication, January 18.

Elisofon, Eliot, and William Fagg
1958 The sculpture of Africa. New York.

Freeman, Richard Austin
1898 Travels and life in Ashanti and Jaman. Westminster.

Gerbrands, A. A.
1957 Art as an element of culture, especially in negro-Africa. Mededelingen van het Rijksmuseum voor Volkenkunde, Leiden, 12.

Ghent. Musée des Beaux Arts
1950 Ars exotica, 7. Septembre—30. Octobre. [Catalogue d'une exposition, introduction par Frans M. Olbrechts] Gand.

Goldwater, Robert
1960 Bambara sculpture from the Western Sudan. New York.

Guillaume, Paul, and Thomas Munro
1926 Primitive Negro sculpture. London.

Himmelheber, Hans
1960 Negerkunst und Negerkünstler. Braunschweig. (Bibliothek für Kunst- und Antiquitätenfreunde, 40)

Holas, B.
1957a Les Sénoufo (y compris les Minianka). Paris. (Monographies ethnologiques africaines)
1957b Note sur la fonction rituelle de deux catégories de statues sénoufo. Artibus asiae, 20, 1:29-35.
1960 Cultures matérielles de la Côte d'Ivoire. Paris.
1962 An annotated glossary of Senufo sculptured objects prepared for "Senufo Sculpture from West Africa," an exhibition organized by The Museum of Primitive Art.

Kjersmeier, Carl
1935 Centres de style de la sculpture nègre africaine, v.1. Afrique Occidentale Française. Paris.

Knops, P.
1956 Contribution à l'étude des Sénoufo de la Côte d'Ivoire et du Soudan. Bulletin de la Société Royale Belge d'Anthropologie et de Préhistoire, 67:141-168.
1958 Aspect de la vie agricole des Sénoufo de l'Afrique occidentale. Bulletin de la Société Royale Belge d'Anthropologie et de Préhistoire, 69:105-129.
1959 L'artisan Sénufo dans son cadre Ouest-Africain. Bulletin de la Société Royale Belge d'Anthropologie et de Préhistoire, 70:83-111.

Knops, P., and J. Weyns
1953 Bijdragen over kunst en kultuur van de Senufo. Bulletin de Musées royaux d'art et d'histoire, Bruxelles, sér. 4, 25:60-71.

Lem, F.-H.
1942 Au sujet d'une statuette sénoufo. Bulletin de l'Institut Français d'Afrique Noire, 4:175-181.
1948 Sculptures soudanaises. Paris.

Leuzinger, Elsy
1960 Africa; the art of the Negro peoples. New York. (Art of the world)
1963 Afrikanische Skulpturen; beschreibender Katalog, African sculpture; a descriptive catalogue, Museum Rietberg. Zürich.

London. British Museum
1953 The Webster Plass collection of African art; an illustrated catalogue by William Fagg. London.

Maesen, Albert
1940 De plastiek in de kultuur van de Senufo van de Ivoorkunst (Fransch West Afrika). [Unpublished doctoral dissertation, University of Ghent]
1962 Communication, July 30.

New York. The Museum of Modern Art
1935 African Negro art [Exhibition catalogue] edited by James Johnson Sweeney. New York.

Pau. Musée des Beaux-Arts
1961 Sculptures de l'Afrique noire; décembre 1961—janvier 1962. [Catalogue d'une exposition par Jacqueline Delange] Pau.

Paulme, Denise
1956 Les sculptures de l'Afrique noire. Paris. (L'Oeil du connaisseur)

Philadelphia. University Museum.
1956 African tribal sculpture; April-September. [Exhibition catalogue] by Margaret Plass. Philadelphia.

Prouteaux, M.
1918-1919 Notes sur certains rites magico-religieux de la Haute Côte d'Ivoire. L'Anthropologie, 29:37-52.

Storrer, Emil
1962 Die Nyi-kar-yi von Watyene. [Unpublished article]

Vandenhoute, P. J. L.
1948 Classification stylistique du masque Dan et Guéré de la Côte d'Ivoire Occidentale (A.O.F.). Mededelingen van het Rijksmuseum voor Volkenkunde, Leiden, 4.
1962 Communication, October 18.

Vendeix, M.-J.
1934 Nouvelle essai de monographie du pays sénoufo. Bulletin du Comité d'Etudes historiques et scientifiques de l'A.O.F., 17, 4:639-641.

Sources of photographs

Africa-Centrum: 40

Art Institute of Chicago: 90, 100

Marc and Evelyne Bernheim from Rapho Guillumette Pictures: 2, 3, 178, 179, 180, 181

Paul Bijtebier: 51, 157

Zoé Binswanger: 80, 81

British Museum: 55, 120

Brooklyn Museum: 124

Buffalo Museum of Science: 106

Dominique Darbois: 21, 60, 69

Walter Dräyer: 141

Eliot Elisofon: 52, 56, 56a, 58, 63, 67, 68, 68a, 84, 85, 85a, 89, 98, 99, 99a

Etnografisch Museum, Antwerp: 29

Walker Evans: 92, 92a, 115, 115a, 122, 122a, 123, 154, 159

Peter Heman: 101

Hans Himmelheber: 164

Michel Huet: 27

Indiana University, Museum of Art: 182, 183, 184

Peter A. Juley & Son: 107

P. Knops, s.m.a.: 1, 4, 5, 7, 16, 17

C. J. Larson: 70

Galerie Le Corneur-Roudillon: 37, 47, 135

Martin Linsey: 119

Elisabeth Little: 6, 25, 28, 32, 34, 36, 38, 45, 49, 65, 72, 74, 77, 83, 86, 87, 88, 88a, 91, 91a, 102, 103, 104, 108, 109, 109a, 112, 116, 125, 128, 128a, 131, 133, 137, 138, 144, 145, 148, 148a, 150, 152, 153, 155, 156, 160, 161, 169, 176, 186

Musée de l'Homme: 42, 121

O. E. Nelson: 96

Arnold Newman: 23, 127

José Oster: 162

István Rácz: 94

Charles Ratton: 22, 130, 142, 165, 171

Museum Rietberg: 151

Rijksmuseum voor Volkenkunde: 30, 39, 53, 61, 185

Rijksuniversiteit, Gent: 129, 166

Seattle Art Museum: 62

Warren Shuman: 71, 79, 79a, 117, 117a

Emil Storrer: 18, 139, 140, 168

Hubert Stout: 41, 46, 134, 134a, 158, 175, 177

Studio Alpy: 48

Henri Tabah: 86a

Taylor & Dull: 76, 87a, 149

Charles Uht: 24, 26, 33, 35, 43, 44, 50, 54, 59, 64, 66, 73, 75, 78, 93, 93a, 95, 110, 111, 113, 114, 126, 136, 143, 146, 147, 167, 170, 173

P. J. Vandenhoute: 31, 105

L. Veroft: 57, 82, 132, 163, 174

Pablo Volta: 172

Rachel Wiberg: 97

Raymond Wielgus: 19, 20, 118, 118a

Source of drawings:

Gilbert Bochet: 8, 9, 10, 11, 12, 13, 14, 15

Map:

William and Caroline Harris